Old Mother Hubbard

A pantomime

Tony Nicholls

Samuel French — London
www.samuelfrench-london.co.uk

©2008 TONY NICHOLLS

Rights of Performance by Amateurs are controlled by Samuel French Ltd, 52 Fitzroy Street, London W1T 5JR, and they, or their authorized agents, issue licences to amateurs on payment of a fee. **It is an infringement of the Copyright to give any performance or public reading of the play before the fee has been paid and the licence issued.**

The Royalty Fee indicated below is subject to contract and subject to variation at the sole discretion of Samuel French Ltd.

Basic fee for each and every
performance by amateurs   Code L
in the British Isles

The publication of this play does not imply that it is necessarily available for performance by amateurs or professionals, either in the British Isles or Overseas. Amateurs and professionals considering a production are strongly advised in their own interests to apply to the appropriate agents for written consent before starting rehearsals or booking a theatre or hall.

The right of Tony Nicholls to be identified as author of this work has been asserted by him in accordance with Section 77 of the Copyright, Designs and Patents Act 1988

ISBN 978 0 573 16451 4

Please see page vi for further copyright information

OLD MOTHER HUBBARD

Based on the script originally produced in November 1988, this revised version was first presented by the Hayman Theatre Company on November 25, 2003 with the following cast:

Hepzibah, The Witch	Sara Green
Her Cat, Astrophe	Sarah Edmunds
Old Mother Hubbard	Josh Price
Polly	Lauren Langlois
Dick	Suzanne Rofe
Woolly Dog	Mimi Leith
Duke Ferdinand	Jez Obern
Ruff	Lawrence Ashford
Scruff	James McGleave
Cloaca, Villager, Cherub	Zoe Cooper
Sybil, Villager, Cherub, Monster, Mookling	Sandra Bahbah
HP, Villager, Cherub, Monster	Fiona Bruce
Little Witch Barbie, Villager, Cherub, Monster, Mookling, Prince Lorien	Samantha Glatz
Queen Mavis, Villager, Cherub, Monster, Mookling	Samantha Young
Leonardo, Villager, Cherub, Monster, Mookling	Andy Harmsen
Faustus, Villager, Cherub, Monster, Mookling	Sophie Dunham
Jack, Cherub, Monster, Mookling	Claire Nichols
Jill, Cherub, Monster, Mookling	Bonnie Parker
Georgy Porgy, Cherub, Monster, Mookling	Nick Arcaro
Miss Muffett, Cherub, Monster, Mookling	Bek Smith
Bo Peep, Cherub, Monster, Mookling	Emma Hayes
Villager, Cherub, Monster, Mookling	Annalise Mack
Sukie, Cherub, Monster, Mookling	Paige Marshall

All other parts played by members of the company

Directed by Tony Nicholls
Music composed and directed by Richard John
Choreography by Claire Nichols
Lighting designed by Duncan A. Sharp
Stage manager – Gabby Pitt

CHARACTERS

Hepzibah, a witch
Astrophe, her cat
Old Mother Hubbard, a dame
Polly, her daughter
Woolly, her faithful dog
Dick, a poor woodchopper's son
Duke Ferdinand, a villain
Ruff, his servant
Scruff, his other servant
Cloaca, an enchantress
Sybil, a wise woman
Leonardo, a Sybil servant
HP, a hidden princess
Lorien, a hidden prince
Little Witch Barbie, a doll
Queen Mavis, Queen of the Witches
Faustus, a gnome-like creature
MC
Jack, a Nursery Rhyme Land character
Jill, a Nursery Rhyme Land character
Bo Peep, a Nursery Rhyme Land character
Sukie, a Nursery Rhyme Land character
2 Dolly Birds

Chorus of People of Nursery Rhyme Land,
Mooklings and Cherubs, etc.

COPYRIGHT INFORMATION

(See also page ii)

This play is fully protected under the Copyright Laws of the British Commonwealth of Nations, the United States of America and all countries of the Berne and Universal Copyright Conventions.

All rights including Stage, Motion Picture, Radio, Television, Public Reading, and Translation into Foreign Languages, are strictly reserved.

No part of this publication may lawfully be reproduced in ANY form or by any means — photocopying, typescript, recording (including video-recording), manuscript, electronic, mechanical, or otherwise—or be transmitted or stored in a retrieval system, without prior permission.

Licences for amateur performances are issued subject to the understanding that it shall be made clear in all advertising matter that the audience will witness an amateur performance; that the names of the authors of the plays shall be included on all programmes; and that the integrity of the authors' work will be preserved.

The Royalty Fee is subject to contract and subject to variation at the sole discretion of Samuel French Ltd.

In Theatres or Halls seating Four Hundred or more the fee will be subject to negotiation.

In Territories Overseas the fee quoted above may not apply. A fee will be quoted on application to our local authorized agent, or if there is no such agent, on application to Samuel French Ltd, London.

VIDEO-RECORDING OF AMATEUR PRODUCTIONS

Please note that the copyright laws governing video-recording are extremely complex and that it should not be assumed that any play may be video-recorded for whatever purpose without first obtaining the permission of the appropriate agents. The fact that a play is published by Samuel French Ltd does not indicate that video rights are available or that Samuel French Ltd controls such rights.

SYNOPSIS OF SCENES

ACT I
SCENE 1	Election Night	Auditorium
SCENE 2	Ejected but not Dejected	Tabs
SCENE 3	Nursery Rhyme Land	Nursery Rhyme Land
SCENE 4	Old Mother Hubbard	Nursery Rhyme Land
SCENE 5	Romantic Revelations	Nursery Rhyme Land
SCENE 6	Duke Ferdinand	Nursery Rhyme Land
SCENE 7	The Lovers Divided	Nursery Rhyme Land
SCENE 8	Sybil	Tabs
SCENE 9	The Youth Machine	Sybil's Necromantic Studio
SCENE 10	The Lost City	Tabs
SCENE 11	Room for Improvement	A Room in The Duke's Castle
SCENE 12	To Flee or Not to Flee	Tabs
SCENE 13	The Kingdom of Love	The Kingdom of Love

ACT II
SCENE 1	In the Badlands	The Badlands
SCENE 2	Cloaca	The Badlands
SCENE 3	Creepy Creatures	The Badlands
SCENE 4	Search for a Maiden	The Badlands
SCENE 5	The Plots Thicken	The Badlands
SCENE 6	Alone	The Badlands
SCENE 7	Polly Escapes	The Badlands
SCENE 8	Last Chance	Tabs
SCENE 9	Friends	Tabs
SCENE 10	The Palace of Arwon	The Palace of Arwon
SCENE 11	An Unlikely Alliance	The Palace of Arwon
SCENE 12	The Great Mookie!	The Palace of Arwon

MUSICAL NUMBERS

ACT I

No 1	Song and Dance	Villagers and Nursery Rhyme Characters
No 2		Polly, Old Mother Hubbard and Woolly
No 3	A Song about Money	Duke Ferdinand, Old Mother Hubbard, Ruff, Scruff and Chorus
No 4		Hepzibah, Astrophe
No 5	Romantic Song and Dance	Dick, Polly, Woolly and Chorus

ACT II

No 6	Badlands Ballet	Mooklings and Assorted Creatures of the Forest
No 7	A Wicked Song	Cloaca and the Mooklings
No 8	Audience Participation Song	Old Mother Hubbard, Chorus and Audience
No 9	Finale	Company

COPYRIGHT MUSIC

The notice printed below on behalf of the Performing Right Society should be carefully read if any copyright music is used in this play.

The permission of the owner of the performing rights in copyright music must be obtained before any public performance may be given, whether in conjunction with a play or sketch or otherwise, and this permissionis just as necessary for amateur performances as for perfessional. The majority of copyright musical works (other than oratorios, musical plays and similar dramatico-musical works) are controlled in the British Commonwealth by the PERFORMING RIGHT SOCIETY LTD, 29-33 Berners Street, London W1P 4AA.

The Society's practice is to issue licences authorizing the use of its repertoire to the proprietors of premises at which music is publicly performed, or, alternatively, to the organizers of musical entertainments, but the Society does not require payment of fees by performers as such. Producers or promoters of plays, sketches, etc., at which music is to be performed, during or after the play or sketch, should ascertain whether the premises at which their performances are to be given are covered by a licence issued by the Society, and if they are not, should make application to the Society for particulars as to the fee payable.

A separate and additional licence from PHONOGRAPHIC PERFORMANCES LTD, 1 Upper James Street, London W1R 3HG, is needed whenever commercial recordings are used.

PRODUCTION NOTES

Structure

Old Mother Hubbard follows conventional pantomime dramaturgy interspersing 'tab scenes' with 'full-stage scenes'. 'Tab scenes' are intended to be performed on the forestage in front of the house curtain while sets are changed out of sight (and sound!) of the audience. They require no specific scenery though atmospheric lighting can be used effectively to suggest mood. At the end of the 'tab scene' the curtain opens on the next 'full-stage' scene thus enabling the action of the show to be continuous.

In Old Mother Hubbard, scenes 2, 8, 10 and 12 in ACT I and scenes 8 and 9 in ACT II may be played as 'tab scenes'. Scene 1 of ACT I can also be staged as a tab scene turning the auditorium into the meeting hall.

Settings

Four sets are required for Act I:

Outside Old Mother Hubbard's house in Nursery Rhyme Land
Inside Sybil's Necromantic Studio
The spare room in the Duke's castle
The Kingdom of Love

Act II requires two sets:

The Badlands
The Ruined Palace of Arwon

Casting

One of the conventions of traditional pantomime is the cross-gender casting of the Dame and the Hero or Principal Boy. Although not absolutely essential it is strongly recommended that this tradition be followed and that Old Mother Hubbard be played by a male actor and Dick by a female. The script has been written with this expectation.

I also like to keep chorus members busy and onstage as much as possible with something interesting and useful to do. The cast breakdown on p.iii shows how we accomplished this in the most recent production.

Tony Nicholls

ACT I

Scene 1

ELECTION NIGHT

The witches, warlocks, MC, and miscellaneous monstrosities, blowing party whistles etc., erupt into the auditorium which for the first scene becomes their meeting place

The MC steps forward

MC Ladies, gentlemen, fellow members of the witches, warlocks and miscellaneous monstrosities union!

All cheer

Pray silence for her graceless majesty, Mavis, queen of all the witches!

All cheer

Queen Mavis enters, waving graciously, clutching an electric frog-squeezer

Queen Thank you, thank you so much! Tonight, I retire as your queen...
All Shame! Shame! Stay! Stay! Etc.
Queen You're very kind but, truly, the time has come for me to hang up my wand, trade in my broomstick for a (*name of current car with silliest name*) and put down fresh roots in pastures new - namely the Witchy-Poo Persons Retirement Village down at Soggy Bottoms.

Cheers

But before I go, proudly clutching this rather wonderful electric frog-squeezer you've so kindly given me, I do have one very pleasant duty to perform which is to announce the name of my successor!

All cheer

May I have the envelope please!

The MC hands her the envelope which she opens

And the nominations are, first, our very own scarlet starlet — Little Witch Barbie!

A glamorous pink Little Witch Barbie comes tottering in on high heels and not much else

Catcalls and whistles

And second — Witch Hepzibah.

The old witch Hepzibah, with her cat - Astrophe, enters eagerly but her reception is less than enthusiastic. Angrily she gestures to her cat who offers a token meow! And raises a placard reading: Hepzibah for queen

Quite. And now I shall announce the name of the lucky winner, that happy creature who will be crowned the new Grand Panjandrum and Queen of all the Witchy-Poo Persons!

All cheer

MC hands Queen Mavis another envelope. Excitement as she opens it

And the winner is — Little Witch Barbie!

Cheers, whistles, screams. Little Witch Barbie is very excited

Barbie What? Me? Really!? This is amazing!— I mean, I never dreamed ...
All Speech! Speech!
Barbie Well, really, this is so unexpected and I'm sure I don't deserve it — well, I suppose I do really because I'm so cool — but I'd like to thank my mum and my dad and my sister Emily and my boyfriend Joshua — hi Josh——
Hepzibah Stop, stop! This is absolutely vomit-making! Who could possibly prefer her to me?
Queen Anyone with an ounce of taste?
Hepzibah But why?
Queen My dear Hepzibah, I should have thought that was obvious

even to you. I mean, on the one hand we have this delightful creature, positively reeking with charm, talent and cheap scent and on the other we have you — a flat-chested old bat with a face with more lines than the London Underground!
Hepzibah Ooh! I've never been so insulted in my life!
Queen That's your own fault, dear — you should get out more.

All laugh

Hepzibah Well, I'd rather look like me than this anorexic clothes-horse with her Brillo Pad hairdo and legs right up to her bottom!
Barbie At least I'm young! I'm not a knobby old antique like you!
Hepzibah Antique! Did you hear that? She called me an antique!
Queen Well, let's face it, dear, you'll never see nine hundred and seventy-five again!
Hepzibah Right, that does it. I'm not standing for this — I'm revolting!
Barbie You said it, sweetie.
Hepzibah You give me that crown right now, do you hear?

Hepzibah hurls herself at Little Witch Barbie. The others and Astrophe intervene. A brief but noisy struggle ensues and Hepzibah and Astrophe are defeated

Queen Come on everyone, we have a party to go to! But not you, Hepzibah — you're banished!

The others exit, leaving Hepzibah and Astrophe

SCENE 2

EJECTED BUT NOT DEJECTED

Hepzibah Banished! Banished! At my age!
Astrophe No. Because of your age.
Hepzibah That's just an excuse!
Astrophe Face facts, Heppy! You're too old. I'm too old. We're both too old! The drunken teenager of time has screamed through and left us mere smears on the great motorway of life. And there's nothing you can do about it!
Hepzibah There is! There must be!
Astrophe Come home and I'll make you a nice supper ...
Hepzibah No.

Astrophe I have cockroach crackles...
Hepzibah Cockroach crackles?
Astrophe And frog yoghourt...
Hepzibah Frog yoghourt?
Astrophe And — a kingsize mouse bar!
Hepzibah You mean Mars Bar.
Astrophe No, I don't!

Astrophe produces a large Mars Bar with a mouse tail hanging out. Hepzibah is unimpressed

Hepzibah Oh, very funny!
Astrophe I was only trying to cheer you up.
Hepzibah Don't bother. I'm sunk too deep in foul despair. The only thing that would cheer me up is something to make me young again.
Astrophe What do you mean 'again'?
Hepzibah Watch it, furbag! Or when I do find a way to make me young again, I'll include you out! And you know what that would mean ... (*Making a throat-cutting gesture*)
Astrophe No!
Hepzibah Yes — it would be the ethnic restaurant for you, kiddo! I mean, you can't have a young witch with an old pussy.
Astrophe How can I make you understand? There is no way in the world you can ever be young — again!
Hepzibah There is! And I am going to find it!

Hepzibah strikes a dramatic pose, then rushes off

Astrophe Oh dear, oh dear. (*To the audience*) This is all going to end in a mess and a mix-up, I just know it. Of course I could just leave her, but she wouldn't last five minutes without me.
Hepzibah (*off*) Astrophe, why has everything gone dark?
Astrophe (*to audience*) Her hat's come down over her eyes again. (*To Hepzibah*) Coming!

Astrophe follows Hepzibah off

Scene 3

NURSERY RHYME LAND

An idyllic landscape of trees, wishing wells, distant hills etc.

To one side is Old Mother Hubbard's cottage

Act I, Scene 3

The CURTAIN *rises on various nursery rhyme characters and other villagers assembled there*

Music No 1

Jack Hello everyone! Welcome to another wonderful morning in Nursery Rhyme Land!

All cheer

I'm Jack and this is Jill and we've all gathered here today especially to——
Jill All of us? Are you sure about that?
Jack Why, is there someone missing?
Jill I think so.

All look about

Jack Who is it?
Bo Peep I know how we can find out!
All How?
Bo Peep By asking whoever's not here to put their hand up!

All groan

Sukie (*to audience*) You can see why she keeps losing her sheep, can't you?
Jill It doesn't matter, anyway. I know who's missing.
All Who?
Jill (*to audience*) You know too, don't you? Who have you come to see today? That's right — Old Mother Hubbard!
All Yes, of course — Old Mother Hubbard!
Jack But where is she?
Jill She can't be far away. Let's all give her a call. (*To audience*) Will you help us? Will you? Right then — I'll count to three and then we'll all shout: 'Old Mother Hubbard'! All right? Are you ready?
All Yes!
Jill One, two, three ...
All Old Mother Hubbard!

All cup ears and listen left

Jack Nothing's happened.
Jill Well, that was such a feeble shout, I'm not surprised. Let's try again

and this time the mums and dads and aunts and uncles and grandmas and granddads can join in. Yes, you can! One, two, three ...
All Old Mother Hubbard!

All cup ears and listen right

Jill Still no good. I think we'd better try just once more. A really good roof-raising roar this time. One, two, three ...
All Old Mother Hubbard!

Scene 4

OLD MOTHER HUBBARD

Hubbard (*at the rear of the auditorium*) Cooee! Did somebody call? (*Appearing in the aisle with a fishing rod*) Hello! Hello!

She greets the audience as she makes her way to the stage

Jack Old Mother Hubbard — where have you been?
Hubbard I was out fishing with (*name of current fishing guru*)
Jill Any good?
Hubbard No, he kept falling off the hook. Ha-ha-ha-ha!

All groan

Jill Anyway, you're here now and that's the main thing. Ladies and gentlemen, girls and boys — may we introduce Old Mother Hubbard!

All cheer

Hubbard Oi, I'll have a little less of the 'old' if you don't mind. I prefer to think of myself as Mature Mother Hubbard.
Sukie Hey, Mother Hubbard, where's your dog?
Hubbard A good question! Woolly? Here (*name of stage manager*) give us that lead!

She goes to the wings and is handed an (elastic) dog lead. She pulls heavily on the lead which stretches across the stage

We went on quite a long walk this morning. He's probably a bit stuffed.

Act I, Scene 4

One last pull and a small stuffed dog on the end of the lead flies on hitting Old Mother Hubbard and knocking her over. She examines it

In fact he's totally stuffed. Wait a minute — this isn't Woolly!

From the rear of the auditorium we hear Woolly

Woolly (*off*) Woof, woof!
Hubbard Aha! That's more like it! I hear the baying of the Hubbard Hound! Will he come that way? (*Indicating right side*) Or will he come that way? (*Indicating left side*)

Woolly appears in the auditorium

There he is! Woolly, Woolly, Woolly! Come to mummy then.

Woolly roams the auditorium happily molesting audience members

Hubbard Woolly — stop that! Don't lick that little boy — you don't know where he's been!
Woolly Woof, woof!
Hubbard Really? (*To the others*) He says it's fun finding out. (*To Woolly*) Just come down here at once!

Woolly runs away

Look at that! One word from me and he does what he likes.
Bo Peep What kind of dog is he exactly?
Hubbard Well, my husband used to say he was a poodle.
Sukie A poodle? Why?
Hubbard Because when he was young he was always leaving little poodles everywhere. Personally, I think there's a bit of shitzu in him — in fact sometimes I think he's full of it!

Woolly bounds over and jumps into Old Mother Hubbard's arms

Down, Woolly, down! Mind you, he's ever so clever.
Jill Really?
Hubbard Oh yes. He was top of his class at school.
Sukie At school?
Bo Peep Woolly went to school?

Hubbard Of course. In fact ... (*Approaching child in the audience*) What school do you go to?
Audience member replies

Well, isn't that spooky! That's where Woolly went!

Woolly is very excited

What's your teacher's name?

Child gives name

Not Mr/Miss——? That was Woolly's teacher too!

Woolly runs and slobbers over child

All right, Woolly, that'll do! You know what happens when you get excited.

Woolly calms down

Now come here and show us your party-piece. No, the nice one!

Woolly sits up straight

Good, now are you ready?
Woolly Woof, woof!
Hubbard Right, this is your starter for ten. What do you call the top of a house?
Woolly Roof, roof!
Hubbard Well done! What was the last name of the three billy goats?
Woolly Gruff! Gruff!
Hubbard Perfectly correct. And finally, what sound does a jet-propelled cat make?
Woolly Meeeeeeeeow!
Hubbard (*to audience*) Told you he was clever.

All applaud

Woolly Woof, woof!
Hubbard Eh? What's that?

Woolly rubs his stomach

Act I, Scene 4   9

Hubbard (*to audience*) What's he saying? Hungry? He's hungry? (*To Woolly*) Are you hungry, Woolly?
Woolly Woof, woof!

Woolly begs expectantly. All look at audience

All Uh-oh!
Hubbard Well, as you've been such a good little doggy-kins, do you know what I'm going to do?
Woolly Woof, woof?
Hubbard No. I'm going to go to my cupboard and get you a nice juicy bone!
Woolly Woof, woof!

Old Mother Hubbard goes into her house

Woolly remains

Jill (*to audience*) Well, we all know what's going to happen now, don't we?
All Mmm!
Jack Let's say it together ...
All Old Mother Hubbard went to the cupboard to get her poor dog a bone——
Woolly Woof, woof!
All But when she got there——
Hubbard (*off*) Aah!
All The cupboard was bare——
Hubbard (*off*) Aaah!
All And so the poor dog had none!
Hubbard (*off*) Aaaaah!

Woolly howls

Old Mother Hubbard staggers on, distraught

Woe! Woe! Woe! (*French accent*) My cupboard——she is bare!

All scream and go into elaborate displays of shock horror. Old Mother Hubbard stops and looks at them

All right, all right! (*To audience*) Really, they're doing more wailing than the Japanese fishing fleet. And what are you all so surprised about anyway? My cupboard's always bare! I walk in my little cottage and everywhere I look it's bare, bare, bare! Makes me feel like Goldilocks. Oh, life is terrible!

She bursts into tears

Bo Peep Why don't you come round to my house and watch *Neighbours*?
Hubbard It's not *that* terrible. It's just that I'm so tired of being poor!
Jack Well, yes, but look on the bright side!
Hubbard Bright side?
Jack You've got your health and your strength and all these good friends about you——
Woolly Woof, woof!
Jill —and Woolly dog too!

Woolly slobbers all over her

Hubbard Quite.
Bo Peep And then of course, you've got your daughter, Polly ...
Hubbard Ah yes — Polly!

Romantic music sting

All sigh as Polly appears in the audience carrying a basket of flowers. She skips her way happily to the stage area as all watch her fondly. She stops when she sees Old Mother Hubbard

Polly Mother? What's the matter?
Hubbard Polly, my child!
Polly What is it?
Hubbard Brace yourself!
Polly Why?
Hubbard It's the cupboard — it's ... it's ...
Polly Bare?
Hubbard Yes!

A big tragic moment from everyone except Polly

Polly So, what's new? It's always bare.
Hubbard Don't you start! I was planning to make you one of my famous boomerang pies.
All Boomerang pies?
Hubbard Yes — they keep on coming back! Ha-ha-ha-ha-ha!

All groan and start to leave

All See you later, Mother Hubbard/Bye, Polly/etc.
Hubbard All right, all right, so it was a cheap joke. (*To audience*) I can't afford expensive ones!

All are gone

Only Old Mother Hubbard, Polly and Woolly remain

Scene 5

ROMANTIC REVELATIONS

Polly Mother, come here and let me give you a cuddle.

They do so. Woolly, left out, looks pathetic

And you too, Woolly!

They have a group hug

There, however bad things may seem, we always have each other!

Music No 2

After the number Polly and Old Mother Hubbard sit on a bench with Woolly lying at their feet

Hubbard You know you are good to me, Polly.
Polly Nonsense!
Hubbard You never complain when there isn't any dinner to eat or any money to buy you a new dress ...
Polly That's because those things don't matter to me.
Hubbard But they should! They should matter! They matter to me. I mean, at my age, I should be settled down in some chic little five-bedroom mansionette somewhere with a home theatre and a spa bath and an upstairs! I've always wanted an upstairs but——
Polly Yes?
Hubbard That's another storey!
Polly Mother! You don't really want all those things.
Hubbard Don't I? Sometimes I think there's nothing I wouldn't do to be — rich!

Sinister music sting

Old Mother Hubbard gives a dark, twisted look

Polly You don't mean that.
Hubbard I do. Do you know, when I went to that cupboard today and found it once again a bone-free zone, something snapped deep inside!
Polly It was probably one of those really big beetles.
Hubbard Not inside the cupboard — in here! (*Indicating her heart*) And it was then that I finally decided——
Polly Decided what?
Hubbard I knew — what I must do — for you, Scooby Doo!
Polly But you don't need to do anything for me.
Hubbard Yes I do! You are going to have all those things I never had! Do you remember when you were little how we used to lie in bed at night and chew the fat. God, it tasted horrible. But then we'd talk about the kind of man you'd marry when you grew up. Do you remember what kind of man that was?
Polly Tall, dark, handsome — and rich! What about it?
Hubbard I've found him!
Polly Don't be silly, Mother. That was just a dream. There's no-one like that round here.
Hubbard Oh no?
Polly For a start nobody round here has any money!
Hubbard Oh no?
Polly No. Well, except for ... (*Realizing*) Oh now, just wait a minute, you said tall!
Hubbard Tallish.
Polly And dark!
Hubbard Darkish. You can do wonders with a dollop of Grecian 2000. (*To audience*) I'm not above a bit of touching up myself.
Polly What about handsome?
Hubbard My dear, beauty lies in the eyes of the beholder. If you keep your eyes shut he's lovely.
Polly So, he's not tall, dark and handsome.
Hubbard No. More of your short, fat and ugly. But he is rich!
Polly I see. Then you can only be talking about one man ...
Hubbard Yes!
Polly It's ...
Hubbard Yes!
Polly It's ...

The villagers come rushing on

Act I, Scene 6

All Duke Ferdinand!

SCENE 6

DUKE FERDINAND

All stand aside as the Duke enters, ideally in some extraordinary vehicle pushed by Ruff and Scruff

The Villagers jeer and boo

Ruff Oi! Stop those jeers!
Jack What about the boos?
Scruff No, he quite likes the booze.
Duke Grrr!

The Duke is confronted by a growling Woolly

Woolly Grr!
Duke Grrr!
Woolly Grrrr!
Duke Grrrrr!
Hubbard Isn't it nice — they speak the same language!

Woolly attacks the Duke

Duke Aaah! Get this mangy mutt off me!
Hubbard Heel, Woolly, heel!
Duke Never mind your heel — try your toe!

Scruff goes to kick Woolly but is restrained by a couple of villagers

Polly Stop it! How can you kick poor Woolly?
Ruff It's easy. You do it like this!

He raises his foot to kick Woolly but Woolly grabs it and bites it

  Aaah!
Bo Peep Well, that was very silly!
Sukie A bite like that ...
Bo Peep You run the risk of rabies!
Sukie Come on, Woolly, we'd better get you to a doctor!

They take Woolly aside

Hubbard Duke Ferdinand, I must apologize. Please ignore these unpleasant peasants.
Duke I shall ignore them with all the ignorance at my disposal.
Hubbard Quite. Now who are these two gentlemen?
Duke This is Ruff——
Woolly Ruff!
Duke — and this is Scruff.
Woolly Scruff!
Duke They're me footmen.
Hubbard They look taller.
Duke They used to be me yardmen.
Ruff / Scruff (*together*) Boom, boom!
Duke Get the baggage!
Ruff / Scruff (*together*) Get the baggage!

They pick up Old Mother Hubbard

Duke Not that baggage! The gift!

They drop Old Mother Hubbard and go off

Hubbard A gift? Oh, Duke Ferdinand, you shouldn't have!
Duke I didn't. It's for your daughter.
Hubbard What?
Duke Only joking, dear lady. I would not presume to offer anything to Polly until everything is settled.
Polly Settled? What's settled?

Ruff and Scruff appear carrying a large, heavy parcel

Duke Ah, the present!
Hubbard Oooh! How exciting! Whatever can it be?
Duke It's a thirty-six piece dinner service!
Hubbard Oooh!
Duke Carry on.

Struggling with each other Ruff and Scruff drop the parcel. A huge amplified crash

> I mean a seventy-two piece dinner service. You blithering idiots! That cost me a fortune!

Act I, Scene 6

Ruff What a fibber!
Scruff It was on special at (*name of local discount store*)
Duke Grrr! Pick it up!

They do so but begin to squabble about who is to carry it

  I'm sorry about this.
Hubbard Oh, Duke, think nothing of it. After all, it's the thought that counts and I've always wanted a——

They drop the parcel again

  — hundred and forty-four piece dinner service.
Duke You brainless boofheads!
Ruff We can't help it!
Scruff It's force of habit——
Ruff \
Scruff / (*together*) We used to work for the post office!
Duke I'll give you can't help it! Here — observe.

He picks up the parcel

  This is the way a gentleman presents that something special to that special someone...

They imitate the Duke as he approaches Old Mother Hubbard in a stately eighteenth-century manner

  Mother Hubbard ...
Hubbard Duke Ferdinand ...
Duke I would be charmed——
Ruff \
Scruff / (*together*) Charmed!
Duke ——and honoured——
Ruff \
Scruff / (*together*) Honoured!
Duke ——and generally chuffed to the eyeballs——
Ruff \
Scruff / (*together*) Eyeballs!
Duke ——if you would condescend to accept this——

Woolly growls and jumps on the Duke's back. The Duke drops the parcel.

Another huge crash

Hubbard Two hundred and eighty-eight piece dinner service? Thank you so much.
Duke It was nothing.
Hubbard Well if it wasn't before it probably is now.

She bends over the parcel to inspect the damage

Duke Polly, my dear, may I say you are looking absolutely ravishing?
Polly No. (*She moves away*)

Mother Hubbard is still bending over the parcel

Duke Mother Hubbard, a word in your ear ... (*Your rear*)
Hubbard Pardon?
Duke Have you had the opportunity to consider my little proposition?
Hubbard Well, yes I have.
Duke And?
Hubbard I think it's a very good idea.
Duke Excellent! And what does Polly think of it?
Hubbard Ah, well, actually I haven't had the chance to——
Polly Think of what?
Hubbard Nothing, Polly——
Polly Mother ...
Hubbard Polly, why don't you go and make us all a nice cup of tea?
Polly What proposition?
Hubbard Or even a nasty cup of tea.
Polly What proposition?
Hubbard Polly — put the kettle on!
All Boom, boom!
Polly Not until you tell me exactly what's going on!
Hubbard Polly! Such disobedience! In front of the Duke too!
Duke That's all right, Mother Hubbard. I like a bit of spirit — in a wife!
All A wife?
Duke Yes — a wife!
Woolly Wife! Wife!
Hubbard Polly, my dear, I know this must come as a bit of a shock——
Duke Eh?
Hubbard — I mean surprise. But just think what lies ahead!
Polly I'm trying not to!
Duke (*pushing Old Mother Hubbard aside*) Leave this to me — "mother". (*To Polly*) My dear, I understand your misgivings.

Act I, Scene 6   17

Polly You do?
Duke Oh yes. You perceive the great gulf between us. You realise you are low and ignorant and female and probably a Labour voter — whereas I am a duke and a man and destined to command. But have no fear; though I may have been born with a silver spoon in my mouth I won't shove it down your throat.
Polly Good.
Duke Ah, my darling! I can see us now, walking down the aisle, arm in arm! The shimmer of pink satin — the hiss of gold velvet — and what will you be wearing?
Polly Nothing.
Duke Suits me, my dear!
Polly I mean I shan't be there!
Hubbard
Duke } (*together*) What?
Polly I'm not going to marry you!

All cheer. The Duke and Old Mother Hubbard are aghast

Duke Oh yes, you are!
All Oh no, you're not!

All encourage the audience to join in

Hubbard
Duke } (*together*) Oh yes, you are!
All Oh no, you're not!
Hubbard
Duke } (*together*) Oh yes, you are!
All Oh no, you're not!
Hubbard Don't listen to her, Duke! She doesn't know what's good for her!
Polly Oh yes, I do!
Hubbard And what's that, pray?
Polly It's Dick!
Hubbard
Duke } (*together*) Dick?

Dick, the woodchopper's son, appears and poses heroically with a huge axe over his shoulder

All Aaah! It's Dick, the poor woodchopper's son!

All cheer

Polly Dick's what I want! He's kind and sensitive and respects my need for personal space to grow as a unique individual. He sees the relationship between two people as a partnership of caring and sharing and always putting the seat down in the toilet!
All Hurray!
Polly And — he has a huge chopper!

Dick raises axe

Hubbard Take no notice, Duke. The size of his chopper is irrelevant. It's the size of his bank account that matters!
Dick It's true, I'm not rich ...

All sigh

But I am honest!

All cheer

And one day, when I've made my fortune, I will be honest *and* rich!

All cheer again

Hubbard And when will that be? This year, next year, sometime, never? The Duke is rich now!
Duke Yes!
Polly But Mother!——
Hubbard No, Polly. It's at times like these that a wise mother remembers that famous old saying.
Polly What old saying?
Hubbard \
Duke } (*together*) A Ferdinand is worth two in the bush!

All groan and boo

Hubbard Which means it's the flick for Dick!
All Oh no, it's not!
Hubbard \
Duke } (*together*) Oh yes, it is!
Dick No, it's not!

Act I, Scene 6

Dick squares up to the Duke

Ruff Take care, boy. The Duke is a champion boxer.
Scruff Yeah. He could beat you with both hands tied behind your back!

All look at him

I mean his back.
Duke Look, sonny, there's no point in trying to defy me. You are but a penniless peasant and I am very, very rich! And when you're very, very rich you always get what you want. And I want her!
Dick Over my dead body!
Duke Certainly. I always mix business with pleasure.

They face up with fists raised. Polly pulls Dick away

Polly Stop that, you big bully!
Hubbard Look, Duke, may I suggest you go back to your castle and I'll try and talk some sense into my daughter.
Duke Good idea. You talk sense to her and I'll talk dollars to you!

All groan

Music No 3

Duke All right, I'm going now.

All cheer

I have to supervise the preparations for the wedding! Ha-ha-ha-ha!

All boo

Grrr!

All boo and jeer

The Duke, Ruff and Scruff exit

SCENE 7

THE LOVERS DIVIDED

Hubbard Well, what charming manners!
Jack He deserves it, Mother Hubbard!
Jill He may be rich but he's mean with it!

All agree

Hubbard You're only jealous!
All What?!
Hubbard Because he's somebody and you're all nobodies!
Bo Peep But surely you won't make Polly marry — that!
Hubbard Polly will do whatever I tell her to do!

All protest loudly at this medieval concept

Right, that settles it! I'm putting my foot down with a firm hand. Clear off, or I'll set the dog on you!
Polly Mother, no——!
Hubbard I mean it! Woolly ...
Woolly Woof?
Hubbard Kill! Kill!

Sinister music sting and lighting

Woolly transforms into a vicious, snarling hound. He advances on the terrified peasantry. At the last moment however he jumps at them and starts slobbering all over them. All laugh

There, I said he'd give you a good licking. (*To Woolly*) Do you call this loyalty? I'd send you to bed without any dinner if we had any dinner.
Polly Mother, please, listen to me. I don't want to marry the Duke.
Hubbard But Polly, I'd have thought you'd have wanted to be rich and have hundreds of servants waiting on you foot and mouth!
Polly But I love Dick.
Hubbard Too bad! No daughter of mine is going to marry into poverty if I can prevent it!
Dick Mother Hubbard, do you mean that if I were rich you'd let me marry Polly?

All look at her searchingly

Act I, Scene 7

Hubbard Well, I might — but you're not rich, are you!
Dick No, but I could be.
Hubbard How?
Dick I could find the lost city of Arwon!
All The lost city of Arwon!
Dick They say there's a great treasure there.
All Treasure!
Hubbard Rubbish!
All Rubbish! Sorry...
Hubbard People have been looking for the lost city of Arwon for hundreds of years! It doesn't exist!
Dick Oh yes it does! And I bet I know where it is!
All Where?
Dick The Badlands!
All The Badlands!

Sinister chord

Polly But, Dick, you can't go there! It's too dangerous!
Dick I'd risk any danger for you, Polly.
Polly But you might be killed!
Dick What is death compared to life without you?
All (*a romantic sigh*) Aaah!
Dick Mother Hubbard, when I find that treasure I'll be even richer than the Duke. I beg you, on my knees, postpone the wedding!

A Victorian tableau. All hang on Old Mother Hubbard's decision

Hubbard No. I cannot gamble Polly's future happiness on this lunatic scheme. She's going to marry the Duke and that's that!

All groan and protest

And, to forestall any further arguments, I'm going to lock her in her room!

She produces a huge key. All gasp in horror

Polly Oh, Dick!
Dick Chin up, Poll! While there's life there's hope!

Dick and Polly kiss. All sigh. Old Mother Hubbard is appalled

Hubbard Well, I never!

Dick No, I don't believe you ever did!
Hubbard Oooh! Get in that house, Polly! And the next time any of you lot see her she'll be a duchess! Na-na-na-na!

Tragic music sting as Old Mother Hubbard drives a tearful Polly indoors

Jill This is terrible.
Jack What are you going to do, Dick?
Dick I don't know. But I'll think of something. That's what men are for!

Heroic sting and spot on Dick as——

——the CURTAIN *slowly falls*

SCENE 8

In front of the tabs

Hepzibah, talking on her phone, hurries in. Astrophe follows

Hepzibah Hello? Jadis, is that you? It's Hepzibah! Hepzibah! How's it hangin' Jadi baby? Look, I need to find a way to make me young again and ... what? Jadi? (*To Astrophe*) How do you like that? She says she can't talk to me because she's in the middle of fighting a lion! I mean, the excuses some people come up with!
Astrophe I know so why don't we just go and——
Hepzibah No!
Astrophe No?
Hepzibah No! We move on to plan B! Knock the curtain.
Astrophe Knock the curtain?
Hepzibah Just do it!
Astrophe All right!

Astrophe knocks on the curtain. A huge echoing knocking sound is heard

Interesting. Who did you say lives here?
Hepzibah Sybil!
Astrophe Ze Bill? Have they left ze Sun Hill then?
Hepzibah Not *The Bill*! Sybil! She'll be able to help me, she's a wise woman.
Astrophe Which explains why she's not answering.

Act I, Scene 9

Hepzibah Knock again.
Astrophe Right.

Astrophe knocks again. This time we hear a loud oink sound followed by a crash

  Interestinger and interestinger.
Hepzibah There's someone in there.
Astrophe Well, let's hope so.
Hepzibah (*calling*) Hello, anybody home?
Sybil (*off*) Go away! I'm busy!

Another huge oink sound followed by a crash

Hepzibah But I want to consult you!
Sybil (*off*) Can't talk now...

Oink sound followed by a crash

Hepzibah It's very important——
Sybil (*off*) Not to me!

Oink sound followed by a crash

Hepzibah I can pay!

Sybil's head pops out through the curtain

Sybil I'll be right with you!

She pops in again

Astrophe But you can't pay.
Hepzibah She doesn't know that.
Sybil (*off*) Leonardo, draw the curtains!

SCENE 9

THE YOUTH MACHINE

The CURTAIN *rises on Sybil's necromantic parlour. She stands holding a tray of sandwiches. Faustus, a gnome-like creature, perches on a stool.*

Leonardo, Sybil's Italian toy boy, stands to one side furiously sketching at an easel

Sybil Sorry about that. I was just testing something.
Astrophe What?
Sybil Well, you know that saying: if pigs had wings they'd fly?
Astrophe Yes ...?
Sybil It's not true.
Astrophe Right.
Sybil Bacon sandwich anyone?
Hepzibah No thanks. Are you Sybil?
Sybil Yes. And this is my servant, Leonardo.
Hepzibah A Sybil servant!
Sybil Yes. He draws the curtains. When you've finished the curtains, Leonardo, you can start sketching the furniture.
Leonardo (*with an Italian accent*) Of course, bellissima!

Faustus has been staring at Astrophe and now moves towards her, peering closely at her neck

Astrophe Get off!
Sybil And this is Faustus.
Faustus Look at her neck, mistress, she has such a beautiful neck!
Astrophe Stop it!
Faustus I am so in love with her neck...
Sybil Faustus!
Faustus I hate you!

Faustus goes back angrily to perch on his stool

Sybil Now, what do you want?
Hepzibah I want to be young again.
Sybil What do you mean 'again'?
Hepzibah Don't you start! Just tell me what to do!
Sybil Very well. Leonardo?

Sybil and Leonardo inspect her closely not to say intrusively then have a brief whispered conversation after which

Sybil Well, in our considered opinion ...
Hepzibah Yes?
Leonardo You needa drastic surgery!
Hepzibah You mean plastic surgery.

Act I, Scene 9

Sybil Oh no, he doesn't.
Leonardo But then there'sa your body!──
Hepzibah My body?
Sybil Yes, I mean, you don't actually live in this, do you?
Hepzibah Yes!
Leonardo (*histrionic exclamation*) Minestrone!
Sybil Quite! (*To Leonardo*) You know if she were a car she'd have to be towed away!

They giggle together

Hepzibah Here, look, I don't need all this aggravation — what I need is rejuvenation! And to get it I'm prepared to go the full monty!
All Aaah!
Sybil I don't think the world's ready for that.
Astrophe Nor do I — come on!

Astrophe tries to drag Hepzibah off

Hepzibah Stop! There must be something!
Leonardo Well-a, if-a you's-a desperate────
Hepzibah I am!
Leonardo There is always ze ...
Sybil No!
Leonardo Yes!
Sybil No!
Hepzibah Yes! What?
Leonardo
Sybil } (*together*) The Youth Machine!

Sybil claps her hands. Dramatic fanfare sting

Two Dolly Birds enter and wheel out the Youth Machine. They do the posing and stroking as featured on all cheap TV game shows

Hepzibah The Youth Machine! What does it do?
Leonardo It-a takes you apart and-a restores-a every bit of you to its original condition!
Hepzibah Whoopee!
Sybil In theory anyway. But it's very experimental, there is some risk.
Hepzibah (*getting into the machine*) I don't care — I'm going to be young! I'm going to be young!
Sybil Well, if you're sure ...
Hepzibah Yes — hit it!

Sybil Very well — stand back!

Sybil indicates to Dolly Birds to press the button. Bubbling noise, music, smoke everywhere

When it clears Hepzibah has vanished

Astrophe What's happened? What have you done to her? Where's she gone?
Sybil That's a very good question.

She opens a flap in the machine. There is the sound of a baby crying. Sybil reaches into the machine, lifts out a baby in a shawl with a very tiny pointed hat

Well, she's certainly gone back to her original condition. Who's going to be mother?

She gives the baby to Astrophe

Astrophe What? This is no good! Who's going to look after her, feed her, change her when she — Yuk! Needs changing!
Sybil I was only following orders!
Astrophe Then zap her forward a couple of years and I can send her to the crèche.
Sybil Sorry — it's all or nothing.
Astrophe Then put her back the way she was!
Sybil But I don't know if it——
Astrophe Do it!

Sybil puts the baby into the machine. Repeat sound and smoke business. Hepzibah emerges with a dummy in her mouth. She spits it out. Hugely relieved, Astrophe embraces her

Hepzibah What happened?
Astrophe You're back — just the way you were!
Sybil Well, almost!
Hepzibah What do you mean?
Sybil She still needs changing.
Astrophe No, she always smells like that.
Hepzibah Are you telling me it didn't work?
Astrophe Yes, so that's that, you gave it your best shot, let's go home and forget all about it.

Act I, Scene 10

Hepzibah No! I have to be young again. There must be someone who can help!
Sybil Well, there may be someone——
Hepzibah Who?
Sybil Cloaca!
Leonardo ⎫
Faustus ⎭ (*together*) Cloaca!
Sybil Sh! Leonardo, draw the curtains——
Leonardo But I've drawn them once! Couldn't I just make a photocopy?
Sybil You haven't invented that yet!
Leonardo (*angry*) Fettuccini!

Leonardo draws furiously and the tabs close leaving Hepzibah, Astrophe, Sybil and Faustus on the forestage

SCENE 10

THE LOST CITY

Hepzibah Now, who is this Cloaca?
Sybil Sh! She's an enchantress. She could help but I must warn you — she's really mean!
Hepzibah Where do I find her?
Sybil Have you heard of the lost city of Arwon?
Hepzibah She lives there?
Sybil Lives there? She put it there!
Astrophe This is not a good idea. Let's go.
Hepzibah Would you abandon me in my hour of need?
Astrophe Just watch me.
Faustus You could stay here! With your neck——
Astrophe Get off!

Faustus goes and checks out the audience's necks

Sybil Or you could help me with my new project.
Astrophe What is your new project?
Sybil Well, you know that saying about cats having nine lives?

Astrophe grabs Hepzibah

Astrophe We're going — now!
Sybil Pity. Faustus, leave those children alone!
Hepzibah Look, I know I'm going to regret this but what is it with him and necks?

Sybil He's a neck romancer.
Hepzibah ⎫
Astrophe ⎭ (*together*) Right!
Sybil Now come on Faustus, we have to go and see that nice Mr Marlowe.

Sybil and Faustus exit

Hepzibah Come on Astrophe, follow me!
Astrophe Where to?
Hepzibah To talk to this Cloaca!
Astrophe Where at?
Hepzibah The lost city of Arwon!
Astrophe And where's that?
Hepzibah Well, it's — it's — lost! Aaaaah! Curses and catspaws! Now what do we do?

She cries on Astrophe's shoulder

Astrophe I think we should go home and have a nice cup of cattucino.
Hepzibah No! Hepzibah never gives up!
Astrophe You gave up washing.
Hepzibah I shall find the lost city of Arwon!

Music No 4

Astrophe That's all very well but even if you find the lost city you've still got to make a deal with this Cloaca creature and Sybil said she was really mean!
Hepzibah Nobody is meaner than me!
Astrophe (*to audience*) She has a point there. (*To Hepzibah*) Off you go then.
Hepzibah Right.
Astrophe But count me out.
Hepzibah What?
Astrophe I'm not coming. If you want to make a fool of yourself you can do it without my help.

Pause. Hepzibah considers a strategy

Hepzibah You're scared.
Astrophe No, I'm not.
Hepzibah Yes, you are!

Act I, Scene 11

Astrophe Not!
Hepzibah Are!
Astrophe Not!
Hepzibah Scaredy-cat! Scaredy-cat!
Astrophe I'm not a scaredy-cat!
Hepzibah Prove it!
Astrophe How?
Hepzibah Come with me!
Astrophe Right!

Pause. Astrophe realizes, turns and addresses audience

Peer group pressure. It's a real bummer.

Hepzibah sniggers and produces a wand

Hepzibah Stand clear!
Astrophe Oh no — not the wand!
Hepzibah What's wrong with it?
Astrophe Tesco's finest? It's about as reliable as (*name of local football team*)
Hepzibah Yah!

Astrophe covers her ears as Hepzibah waves her wand

Spirit of mischief, greed and malice — transport us to the old lost palace!

There is a flash and a bang. The tabs opens on

Scene 11

ROOM FOR IMPROVEMENT

A room, dingy and dirty, with a scruffy carpet or dust cover on the floor

Astrophe Where are we?
Hepzibah The lost palace of Arwon!
Astrophe I don't think so.
Hepzibah Why not?
Astrophe It doesn't look like a lost palace. It looks more like a spare room in the Duke's castle in Nursery Rhyme Land which is about to be redecorated as a bridal chamber.

Hepzibah What makes you say that?
Astrophe Call it feline intuition.
Hepzibah Well let's go and see, shall we?

Hepzibah strides off and exits L or R

Astrophe But — oh, what's the use?

Astrophe exits after her

Music

The Duke enters from the opposite side followed by a line of servants carrying boxes. The biggest servant should naturally carry a tiny box while the smallest staggers under a huge one

Duke Come on, hurry up! Put them down over there!

They put the boxes down and stand there

What are you waiting for?
Servant 1 What about our money?
Duke Money? You want your money?
Servants Yeh!
Duke Really. And I'd expect you'd like a tip, wouldn't you?
Servants Yeh!
Duke Yeh! Well, here's a tip — always get the money before you do the work! Now, clear off! (*He drives them off*)

The servants exit

Ruff and Scruff enter from the other side with buckets

Ah, there you are! Welcome to the honeymoon suite!
Ruff ⎫
Scruff ⎬ (*together*) Where's that?
Duke (*indicating room*) Da-da!

Ruff and Scruff look at each other and turn to exit

Come back!
Ruff But, Duke, you can't be serious, this is the grottiest room in the castle!
Duke Rubbish! It's got real——

Act I, Scene 11

Scruff Woodworm?
Duke — potential! It just needs a complete——
Ruff Demolition?
Duke — makeover!
Scruff Oh, you mean like changing rooms!
Duke Something like that — but cheaper. A lot cheaper. (*To audience*) I don't usually waste money paying people to clean up——
Ruff and Scruff (*to audience*) We know.
Duke — but this is the last time I shall ever have to do so!
Ruff Eh?
Scruff How do you work that out?
Duke Because, when I'm married, I'll have a wife to do it for me — for nothing! Ha-ha-ha-ha-ha-ha!
Ruff So that's what this is all about.
Scruff He's not such a fool as he looks.
Duke But if Polly finds this place looking like a pigsty, she might think——
Ruff That you're a pig?
Scruff You can see her point.
Duke I want this place looking so clean you could eat your dinner off it!
Scruff Looks as if someone's been doing that already.
Duke Shut up! Why do I surround myself with idiots?
Ruff Because it makes you look cleverer.
Duke Oh yes, that was it. (*To audience*) You know, if I wasn't so mean, I could afford proper servants. (*He cries*)
Ruff There, there, Duke! Fear not! I give you my word as an inveterate liar that when you return you won't be able to believe your eyes.
Duke (*to audience*) That's what I'm afraid of!

Ruff guides the Duke off

Scruff (*checking the things in the boxes*) Lots of good stuff in here.
Ruff Oh yeh?
Scruff (*handing items to Ruff*) Yeh, there's wallpaper ...
Ruff Wallpaper.
Scruff Paste ...
Ruff Paste.
Scruff Parrot food ...
Ruff Parrot food. Parrot food?
Scruff Yes look — polyfilla!
Ruff Idiot! This isn't parrot food! This is for filling nasty cracks. And one more nasty crack out of you and that's what I'll use it for!
Scruff Sorry.

Ruff Didn't you ever go to school?
Scruff Of course I did.
Ruff What school did you go to?
Scruff (*names local girls' school*) had a wonderful time there too.
Ruff But that's a girls' school!
Scruff I told you I had a wonderful time.
Ruff (*handing bucket to Scruff*) Take this.
Scruff What is it?
Ruff Water. If we're going to hang wallpaper we'll need to mix some paste.
Scruff Awesome! Can I mix it, please, can I?
Ruff No! I'll mix it — but you can do the water.
Scruff Coolerama! What do I have to do?
Ruff It's quite simple. I'll stir the paste and when I nod my head — you pour the water on.
Scruff When you nod your head, I pour the water on?
Ruff Yes.

Ruff puts powder in the bucket and stirs. Scruff is worrying

Scruff Er, just checking. When you nod your head, I pour the water on?
Ruff How many more times? Yes!
Scruff Just wanted to be sure, that's all.
Ruff That's all right. Are you ready?
Scruff Yes.
Ruff Now!

Ruff nods his head. Scruff pours water over it

  You idiot! What did you do that for?
Scruff I thought——
Ruff You never think — that's your trouble!
Scruff I'm sorry, I'm sorry, I'm sorry ...
Ruff We're never going to get this finished in time!
Scruff Yes, we will. What does Bob the Builder say? Can we fix it?
Ruff }
Scruff } (*together*) Yes, we can!
Scruff Right. You hold the wallpaper up and I'll paste it.

NB. The 'wallpaper' in this scene is actually a length of painted calico or stage canvas

Ruff holds the wallpaper up in front of him as Scruff starts to apply paste to it

Act I, Scene 11

As he does so, Hepzibah and Astrophe enter, cross the stage and exit the other side

Scruff notices something but is not sure what. He stops pasting to look. Ruff lowers the paper

Ruff What have you stopped for?
Scruff Nothing.

Scruff turns back and slaps paste brush into Ruff's face

Ruff Ooogh! What did you do that for?
Scruff I'm sorry — I thought I saw a witch!
Ruff A what?
Scruff No, a witch!
Ruff Rubbish. Now stretch the paper out so we can check the length.

They turn paper sideways and stretch it out across the stage

How long do you think it is? How many feet?

Hepzibah's feet appear walking behind and below the paper

Scruff Er — two!
Ruff Rubbish, it's more than two feet!

Astrophe's feet appear following Hepzibah

Scruff You're right — it's four feet!
Ruff What?
Scruff And they're kicking each other!

Scruff points at the feet. We hear violent whispering. They lower the wallpaper to reveal Astrophe trying to drag Hepzibah off

All Aaargh!

Ruff and Scruff panic and roll themselves up in the wallpaper

Hepzibah and Astrophe go to flee but hear the Duke returning

Duke (*offstage*) Ruff! Scruff!

Hepzibah and Astrophe turn and flee off L

The Duke enters R

He looks at Ruff and Scruff and the room

  Pleased with progress, are you?
Ruff Oh yes.
Scruff We're rapt.
Duke Grrr! You haven't done a thing!

Ruff and Scruff release themselves from the wallpaper

Ruff We can explain ...
Scruff There was a witch——
Duke A what?
Ruff ⎫
Scruff ⎬ (*together*) No, a witch!
Duke Rubbish! There's no such thing as witches!

Hepzibah re-appeares L, *being held back by Astrophe*

The Duke sees her

Hepzibah Sorry to trouble you but we're looking for the——
Duke Aaargh!

Hepzibah is dragged off by Astrophe

  That was a witch!
Ruff ⎫
Scruff ⎬ (*together*) We know!
Duke Right, I'll soon fix her! (*He picks up a bucket and heads for the* L *entrance*)

Hepzibah appears R

Hepzibah I just want to——
Ruff This side! This side!
Duke Aha!

The Duke turns quickly, Hepzibah disappears and he throws water over Ruff

Act I, Scene 11

Ruff Aaah!

Ruff shakes the water off, picks up another bucket and throws water at the Duke who ducks and the contents hit Scruff. Scruff seizes another bucket, hurls water at the Duke who ducks again and the contents hit Ruff

The Duke laughs at their wetness

Ruff and Scruff seize two more buckets which are clearly brimfull of water and approach the Duke who retreats protesting into the auditorium. Ruff and Scruff pursue him round behind the seats on either side

The Duke reappears, still pursued by Ruff and Scruff. He runs down and hides amongst the audience. Ruff and Scruff advance with buckets held high. As the Duke cringes and cries they empty the buckets over him and the audience. The buckets have been switched and now fortunately contain only torn paper

Duke Idiots! Get this mess cleared up before——

Mother Hubbard rushes in

Ruff and Scruff clean up room

Hubbard Duke! Terrible news!
Duke What?
Hubbard It's Dick — he's run off!
Duke Hurray!
Hubbard With Polly!
Duke What! Do you mean that bony beanpole has bolted with me bride-to-be?
Hubbard Probably. One minute she was locked in her room and the next, there she was — gone!
Duke Where to?
Hubbard I don't know but the silly boy was talking about going to find the lost city of Arwon!

Hepzibah and Astrophe appear US *unseen by the others*

All The lost city of Arwon?
Hubbard Yes! He was saying there's a great treasure there and he knows where it is.

Duke (*aside*) Treasure! (*Aloud*) Where is it?
Hubbard The Badlands!
All The Badlands?
Hubbard Yes!
Duke Mother Hubbard, we must pursue it — I mean them — with all possible speed!
Hubbard O Duke, you noble creature! Braving without a thought all that terrible danger to rescue the woman you love!
Duke Danger?
Hubbard The Badlands, you know. Who knows what foul and fearsome fiends frolic through its fusty foliage...
Duke Ha! It takes more than a few frolicking fiends to frighten me! Come on!

All turn and see Hepzibah and Astrophe

All Aaargh!

All scatter in terror as——
—*the* CURTAIN *falls*

SCENE 12

TO FLEE OR NOT TO FLEE

Dick and Polly hurry in

Polly Dick?
Dick Yes?
Polly Are you sure we're doing the right thing? It feels like running away.
Dick We are running away.
Polly That's what it feels like.
Dick Polly, what exactly do you mean?
Polly Well, I'm very grateful to you of course for freeing me from durance vile but I do rather feel as if I'm letting my mother down.
Dick I think she's letting you down, trying to marry you off to that pukey dukey!
Polly I know she is an unenlightened dupe of the prevailing patriarchal system but she's only doing what she thinks is best for me. And who knows, perhaps she's right. Perhaps love isn't as important as I thought. Perhaps I'm being selfish.
Dick Selfish?
Polly Yes. You see, ever since I was a baby my mother has done everything for me. She's fed me, clothed me, changed my nappies ...

Act I, Scene 12

Dick But I want to do that for you now!
Polly Yes, but you see I feel it's my turn to do something for her. That's what I mean by running away. I'm running away from my responsibilities to Mother.
Dick But Polly, you also have a responsibility to yourself. And to me. And there comes a time, old chap, when you have to decide which is the more important.
Polly I understand that, but it doesn't make it any easier. How does one choose between what is right and what is politically correct?
Dick Better men than you have agonized over that one, Poll.
Polly So what should I do?
Dick Well, it's your decision of course but I would just point out that once we've found the treasure not only will we be able to get married but also you'll be able to use some of our new-found riches to buy your mother all the things she's ever wanted!
Polly Yes, that's true! But are you really sure about this treasure?
Dick Absolutely! My grandmother used to tell me stories about it. Long ago there was a city called Arwon. Everything there was made of gold and silver and diamonds!
Polly No!
Dick Yes! The young prince was promised in marriage to a fair princess but he discovered that she was really an evil enchantress with a heart of ice!
Polly No!
Dick Yes! So he sent her away and made plans to marry the lady he really loved. But, on their wedding day, the enchantress returned. She was so jealous of their love she cast a spell that sent the city spinning away into the depths of a dark forest!
Polly What about the prince and princess? What happened to them?
Dick They say she turned them both into — monsters!
Polly No!
Dick Yes! But ever since that day the legends have spread of a lost city filled with treasure; many men have gone to look for it but none have ever succeeded!
Polly That's not very encouraging, Dick.
Dick Perhaps not. But you see I have something that none of those other men had. (*Thrusting his chest out stoutly*)
Polly What's that, Dick?
Dick They went to search for the treasure out of greed but I'm going — out of love!
Polly Oh, Dick!
Dick It's the strongest, surest thing there is. We may be heading off into a land of darkness, danger and far too many scene changes but, when

the chips are down and the last man's in, it's the only thing you can really count on.

They embrace

The tabs open on Woolly and the Chorus in the cupid-ridden dream vision of

Scene 13

THE KINGDOM OF LOVE

Music No 5

Dick Come on, Woolly — to the treasure!
All The treasure!

Dick, Polly and Woolly link arms and set off on their quest as rose petals and hearts fall and the chorus wave tearful goodbyes

On this heroic and inspiring vision——

—the Curtain *slowly falls*

ACT II

Scene 1

IN THE BADLANDS

The CURTAIN *rises on a magical, mysterious forest*

Music No 6

A ballet of Mooklings and assorted creatures of the forest

As the dance ends there is a deep rumbling sound and all flee

Dick enters cautiously followed by Polly and Woolly

Polly Wait — what was that?
Dick Some kind of ballet I think.
Polly No, that rumbling noise——

The deep rumbling sound comes again. They huddle together

Dick I don't know. Now, come on, we have to find that treasure.

They hurry off

Scene 2

CLOACA

We hear the sound of alternating thumps and miaows

Hepzibah and Astrophe enter, the latter rubbing her head and complaining

Hepzibah All right, all right, all right! I apologize! But it was your idea.
Astrophe My idea? All I said was this cave isn't big enough to swing a cat in! I didn't think you'd try and do it!

Hepzibah You shouldn't make these rash statements if you're not prepared to back them up!
Astrophe What?
Hepzibah And after all, you were proved to be perfectly correct. You should be pleased.
Astrophe It's a bit hard to feel pleased when your tail's been yanked by the roots!
Hepzibah Better than the other way round.
Astrophe Yes, thank you!
Hepzibah Just stop whingeing and keep looking!
Astrophe But there's nothing here! We've gone from one end of the Badlands to the other and we haven't seen a soul!
Hepzibah Cloaca has to be here somewhere! (*Her hands have a sudden spasm*) Aaargh!
Astrophe What is it?
Hepzibah Pricking in my thumbs!
Astrophe What does it mean?
Hepzibah I don't know. I usually put it down to bad circulation.

HP, a strange misshapen figure, appears briefly

Aaargh! What was that?
Astrophe What was what?
Hepzibah That creature over there!
Astrophe There's no creature over there. You're losing your marbles.
Hepzibah My marbles are in perfect condition. In fact they're marbellous.

HP appears again

Look!

HP moves forward

Hepzibah }
Astrophe } (*together*) Aaargh!

The creature makes strange mewing sounds. She is trying not to frighten them but they don't realize

Hepzibah Go away! Clear off, you horrible little beast!

Thunderclap

Cloaca appears with the Mooklings

Act II, Scene 2   41

Cloaca HP! Back!

HP retreats

Hepzibah Thank you. May one enquire whom one has the honour of addressing?
Cloaca My name is Cloaca.
Hepzibah Cloaca! Cloaca! It's her! It's her! We've found her! We've found her! (*Leaping about in wild excitement*)
Cloaca Who are you? And what are you doing in the Badlands?
Hepzibah O great enchantress! I am the witch Hepzibah and this is my cat, Astrophe.
Astrophe Miaow.
Hepzibah I come in search of my youth!
Cloaca Well, he hasn't passed this way.

The Mooklings cackle madly at this as they do at all Cloaca's jokes

Hepzibah I mean I want to be young again!
Cloaca What do you mean "again"?
Hepzibah Look, will you cut that out? It's bad enough with her insulting my face right under my nose!
Cloaca Under your nose is where most of it is.
Hepzibah Oooh!
Cloaca Just state your business!
Astrophe Look, let's get this over really quickly, shall we? This daft old biddy thinks that you can make her young. Again. Just tell her she's wasting her time and you can't help her and we'll be off home.
Cloaca Your cat is right.
Astrophe See?
Cloaca I can't help you.
Hepzibah What?
Cloaca But the Great Mookie can!
Mooklings Mookie!
Hepzibah \
Astrophe / (*together*) Who's the Great Mookie?
Cloaca What do you think, HP? Shall we tell them?

HP moans

I'm afraid I have to, my dear. (*To Hepzibah*) The Great Mookie is — a monster!

Hepzibah Errgh!
Cloaca He lives here, deep in the ruins of the lost palace of Arwon. For most of the year he lies sleeping while I and the Mooklings and HP watch over him. But once a year, he wakes up. Now, do you know what he does then?
Hepzibah Well, when I get up, the first thing I do is go for a——

All look at her

—bowl of Coco Pops.
Cloaca Coco Pops? We are talking of the Great Mookie! He doesn't eat Coco Pops!
Hepzibah Fruit loops?
Cloaca He eats pure young maidens!
Hepzibah Aaaah!

She clings in terror to Astrophe

Astrophe What's the matter? We're safe.
Hepzibah Why does he do this?
Cloaca Because if he doesn't get a maiden to eat, he will die!
Astrophe I can relate to that. I feel the same way about mouse-flavoured Whiskas.
Hepzibah Shut up! (*To Cloaca*) What's all this got to do with me?
Cloaca Well, as you know, pure young maidens aren't as plentiful as they used to be. So the Mookie rewards anyone who can supply the necessary article by granting their dearest wish.
Hepzibah You mean ...?
Cloaca Yes! Get the Mookie a maiden and he'll make you young — again!
Hepzibah Ha-ha-ha-ha-ha-ha! (*Capering with joy then realising*) Wait a minute — where am I supposed to get hold of a pure, young maiden?
Cloaca Around the waist?
Hepzibah Oh yes, very funny!
Cloaca If you really want to be young again, I've told you what to do. But I suggest you hurry——

The deep rumbling sound comes again

Hepzibah
Astrophe } (*together*) Aaah! What's that?
Cloaca It's the Great Mookie.
Mooklings Mookie!

Act II, Scene 3

Cloaca He stirs in his sleep. Very soon he will awake and, when he does, he'll be wanting his breakfast. Won't he, HP?
HP howls

So, be off with you! And don't dare return empty-handed! Sometimes the Mookie likes to chew old bones for roughage!
Hepzibah Aaargh!
Cloaca Go!

Hepzibah and Astrophe run off

HP moans

What's the matter, HP? Don't you want the Mookie to eat the maiden?

HP moans, shakes head

Cloaca But if he doesn't he will die!

HP howls piteously at this frightful prospect

Bit of a dilemma for you, isn't it? But don't worry. They'll get him a maiden all right. Or if they don't, someone else will. Selfishness ...
Mooklings Selfishness!
Cloaca Greed ...
Mooklings Greed!
Cloaca There are no more powerful forces in the universe! Except one, of course. True love.
Mooklings Yuk!
Cloaca Whatever happened to that?

Music No 7

The song ends, the Mookie rumbles, HP moans

Cloaca All right, my Mookie, be patient! There's a tasty morsel on its way! Ha-ha-ha-ha-ha-ha!

Cloaca sweeps off followed by HP and the Mooklings

Scene 3

CREEPY CREATURES

Another part of the Badlands

Old Mother Hubbard marches on, followed by the Duke, Ruff and Scruff

Hubbard Halt!

They do so but Scruff keeps going and cannons into the others. All yell loudly and then shh each other

Duke Shut up! What have we stopped for?
Hubbard I heard something.
Duke What?
Hubbard Listen!

The deep rumbling comes again

  Hear that?
Duke I thought it was your stomach.
Hubbard My stomach? What made you think that?
Duke Just a gut reaction.
Scruff Let's go home!
Hubbard What? Go home when my poor Polly is out here somewhere, wandering in this terrible place, all alone?
Ruff She's not alone — the boy's with her.
Scruff And the dog.
Hubbard Ha! What can a mere boy and a dog do against the creepy creatures of the Badlands? They've got about as much chance of survival as a female newsreader with crowsfeet.
Duke Creepy creatures? What creepy creatures?
Hubbard All kinds of creepy creatures. Everything which has been cast out from the world of real people sooner or later finds its way here. It's a morass of moronity, a jungle of junk.

This moment in the show is your opportunity to introduce and send up some of your local irritating people, TV personalities, excruciating ads, appalling pop singers etc. NB it's probably best to attack two or three targets sharply and briefly. Or of course you can just continue with the script

Act II, Scene 3

Scruff Look out!

A half-eaten and gangrenous meat pie appears R

All Aaaah!

A huge ear appears L

Aaaah!
Duke What is it?
Hubbard Don't worry. When you're out in the wilds you often come across the remains of an old pioneer. (*Pie 'n' ear*)

Sudden dinosaur-type roaring off stage. The pie and ear run off in panic

Scruff Wow! Something really scared them.

Roaring again

Hubbard Oh no!
Duke Sounds like a brontosaurus.
Hubbard It's worse than that!
Ruff A tyrannosaurus?
Hubbard Worse than that! There's only one thing that scares a meat pie — apart from a health inspector ...
All No!
Hubbard Yes — it's a tomatosaurus!

A huge bottle of tomato sauce enters. All yell and hide and it goes off after the pie

Duke Let's get out of here.
Scruff Good idea!
Ruff Yes, we don't want that to ketchup with us!

All groan and start to leave

Hubbard Stop! We're supposed to be looking for Polly, remember?
All Oh yes.
Hubbard If only we could get our hands on a clue.
Duke (*checking the sole of his shoe*) Did you say she had the dog with her?

Hubbard Yes.
Duke Then I think I have got my hands on a clue. (*Wiping his hands on Ruff*) They definitely passed this way.
Hubbard Then what are we waiting for? Polly!

They all hurry off

SCENE 4

SEARCH FOR A MAIDEN

The deep rumbling sound is heard again

Hepzibah and Astrophe enter

Hepzibah Astrophe, stop! This is hopeless! Where are we going to find a pure, young maiden?
Astrophe Search me.
Hepzibah Don't be revolting.
Astrophe Why don't you face facts? We are never going to find a maiden in a place like this!
Hepzibah But if we don't I'll never be young again!

She cries on Astrophe's shoulder

Astrophe Come on, now. It's not the end of the world, you know. You still have me.
Hepzibah (*looking up suddenly*) You! Of course! (*Seductively*) How do you look in a white nightie?
Astrophe What? (*She realizes*) Oh no — don't even think about it!
Hepzibah Huh! Some friend you are! Won't even do a simple thing like dress up as a maiden and get eaten by a Mookie!
Astrophe How would you like it?
Hepzibah I don't have to like it. I'm not going to do it!
Astrophe You're so selfish! You don't care what you do to people as long as you get what you want!
Hepzibah Me? Selfish? How dare you!

She attacks Astrophe. Voices are heard approaching. They freeze

    What was that?
Astrophe Voices.

Hepzibah Quick!

They run off

Dick and Woolly enter, supporting Polly

Dick We'll stop here, Woolly. Poor old Polly's just about done in.

They lower Polly to the ground

Polly Oh, Dick, I'm sorry to be such a nuisance.
Dick Not your fault, old girl. I shouldn't have set such a cracking pace.
Polly I'll be all right if I can just rest for a moment.
Dick Of course you can. I mean, the treasure's been there for hundreds of years; I don't suppose another hour's going to make much difference. Take all the rest you need.
Polly Thank you, Dick. (*She lies down and goes to sleep*)
Dick (*taking Woolly aside*) Look, Woolly, I'm afraid I told Polly a bit of a fib just now.
Woolly Woof?
Dick Yes, we don't really have time to rest.
Woolly Woof?
Dick No, you see I've just remembered that I told Old Mother Hubbard about going to find the treasure in the Badlands. Once she finds us missing she's bound to put two and two together and I'm very much afraid she'll make it four!
Woolly Woof, woof!
Dick Yes, then she and the Duke and his men will come after us. If they catch us before we find the treasure they'll take Polly away and marry her to the Duke *toute de suite*!
Woolly Grrr!
Dick So, as Polly's just too whacked to go on, I suggest that I do a bit of exploring — alone!
Woolly Woof, woof!
Dick No, you can't. You've got to stay here and look after Polly.
Woolly Woof!
Dick It's a grave responsibility, Woolly. Can I trust you?
Woolly Woof!
Dick (*thumping Woolly on the back*) Bully, Woolly! You know, sometimes I think that in your dumb doggy sort of way, you love Polly nearly as much as I do.
Woolly Woof!

Dick Carry on!

Both salute

Dick strides off heroically

Woolly assumes a sentry position and begins to march back and forth across the stage

Hepzibah and Astrophe appear upstage behind a tree

Hepzibah Look, a maiden!
Astrophe Where?
Hepzibah There! Come on!
Astrophe But you can't just kidnap her!
Hepzibah Just get that dog out of the way and you'll see what I can do!
Astrophe How do I do that?
Hepzibah You're a cat — he's a dog! Get out there and let nature take its course!
Astrophe But——
Hepzibah Move it!

She shoves Astrophe downstage right into the dog's path. They face each other, frozen. Then Woolly charges, barking. Astrophe retreats hissing. They circle a couple of times then

Woolly chases Astrophe off. The noise of barking and spitting fades away.

Hepzibah watches them go

That's it! You've got his attention, now keep running — good! Mind your tail — mind your ... Oh well, never mind, I'm sure it'll grow back.

The noise has woken Polly up

Polly What was that — where am I — who are you?
Hepzibah Have no fear, my dear. You probably feel a little confused——
Polly Where's my Dick?
Hepzibah Obviously more than a little confused ...
Polly If you've harmed a hair of his head——

Act II, Scene 4

Hepzibah He's gone!
Polly Gone where?
Hepzibah Er — where do you think?
Polly To the palace?
Hepzibah That's it — he's gone to the palace!
Polly You mean he's found it? The lost palace of Arwon?
Hepzibah As ever was. He asked me to come back and take you to him.
Polly Really?
Hepzibah Yes, it's this way.

She goes to lead Polly off

Astrophe hurtles on minus her tail

Astrophe Quick, quick — he's after me!

Astrophe runs off

Polly What? Who was that? What's going on?
Hepzibah I'll tell you later. Come on!

She grabs Polly and hauls her off, protesting

Woolly enters swinging Astrophe's tail and looking very pleased with himself. Then he notices Polly is gone. He is suddenly worried, looks around then sinks down and howls in grief and despair

Dick runs on

Dick Woolly! What's all the noise about?

Woolly goes into a charades routine which Dick interprets

There was a cat. You chased the cat. You beat the cat? Well done! What happened then?

Woolly draws a many-sided figure in the air

Polygon? (*Realizing*) Polly gone! (*Looking at the place where she was sleeping*) No! I don't believe it! Woolly, I hope you're not handing me some kind of tale!

Woolly offers the cat's tail

Woolly Woof!
Dick Aaah! We must get after her at once!

HP enters

Dick and Woolly turn to go but meet HP

Look out!

Woolly growls. HP moans and retreats

Wait, Woolly, it's very peculiar-looking but one shouldn't judge by appearances. I have a funny sort of feeling it's friendly ...

HP nods eagerly

And it seems to understand what we're saying! (*To HP*) Have you seen Polly?

HP nods eagerly

Where is she?

HP indicates direction

Right! Let's go!
Woolly Woof, woof!
Dick What's the matter?
Woolly Woof, woof!
Dick You don't trust her? You think it's a trap? Well, you could be right, of course, but there's something about this little blighter ... (*Making a decision*) No, we have to take the chance! Lead on, McFluff! Take us to Polly and this Crunchie bar is yours!

They exit

Scene 5

THE PLOTS THICKEN

Scruff enters warily

He is carrying a long bough like a lance

Scruff What a place! Scout ahead, says the Duke. If there's any danger you can warn us and we can be prepared. Huh! What he means is that

Act II, Scene 5   51

if he hears me and Ruff being eaten by some scrofulous monster, he'll have time to get away before it eats him!

Ruff enters behind him

Ruff Hey, Scruff——
Scruff Aaah!

Scruff turns quickly and the bough catches Ruff in the stomach

Ruff Ooof!

Ruff seizes the bough and pushes it away from him. This sends Scruff spinning round and the other end of the bough hits Ruff in the back

Aaah!

Ruff is knocked to the floor. Scruff gets into a panic, spinning this way and that with Ruff trying to get up as the bough swings to and fro over his head. Finally he catches it

Stop! Stand still!

Ruff gets up

Now, put the bough down.
Scruff But it's my weapon!
Ruff Put it down!
Scruff But——
Ruff Down!

Scruff drops the bough. It lands on their feet. They both roar and hop about

Stop that! Pull yourself together!

Scruff does so

Now, have you found anything?
Scruff No, but I heard something!
Ruff What?
Scruff (*looking furtively about*) Tweet tweet, tweet tweet, tweet tweet, tweet tweet, tweet tweet!
Ruff Tweet tweet, tweet tweet, tweet tweet, tweet tweet, tweet tweet?

Scruff Tweet tweet, tweet tweet, tweet tweet, tweet tweet, tweet tweet!
Ruff What does it mean?
Scruff I don't know. A little bird told me.
Ruff You fool!

Ruff goes to hit Scruff but hears a noise off

What was that?
Scruff I don't know! Where's me weapon? (*Picking up the bough*)
Ruff What about me? I'm defenceless!

Ruff tries to wrestle the bough from Scruff who resists. They squabble and Ruff begins to swing Scruff round on the end of the bough.

The Duke enters just in time to catch Scruff as he flies off the end

All Aaah!

The Duke drops Scruff

Scruff Aaah!
Duke (*to Ruff*) What's the matter with him?
Ruff I don't know. He just flew off the handle.
Duke Grrr! Now quickly — I've left Old Mother Hubbard up the track. What have you found?
Ruff }
Scruff } (*together*) Er ...
Duke Have you found anything at all?
Ruff Well, yes——
Duke Yes?
Ruff — and no.
Scruff Mainly no.

The Duke appears to be about to explode. They cringe away in expectation of a beating but unexpectedly the Duke smiles

Duke I see. That's a shame. But I expect you're a bit tired, aren't you?
Ruff }
Scruff } (*together*) Well ...
Duke And perhaps a trifle hungry?
Ruff }
Scruff } (*together*) Well ...
Duke And perhaps just a teensy-weensy bit scared of this nasty-wasty old forest?

Act II, Scene 5   53

Ruff
Scruff } (*together*) Well ...

They have relaxed a little. The Duke puts his arms protectively round their shoulders

Duke My poor little boysie-woysies! Come to daddy-waddy..!

They snuggle up to him and pop their thumbs in their mouths. Suddenly the Duke erupts and clashes their heads together

All Aaaaah!
Duke (*angrily flinging them aside*) Now start looking properly!
Scruff But——
Duke No buts! Just find him! Go!

They make to leave, realize and stop

Ruff
Scruff } (*together*) Him?
Ruff I thought we were looking for your fiance?
Duke That's who Old Mother Hubbard is looking for. I want — the boy!

Ruff and Scruff exchange 'looks' and then step away from the Duke

The treasure, you fools! The boy knows where it is!
Ruff Rubbish!
Scruff He'll never find it!
Duke Don't be so sure of that. He's just the sort of goody-goody hero type who always finds lost treasures!
Ruff
Scruff } (*together*) True.
Duke So, first we find him, then we follow him and when he finds the treasure — we pounce!
Ruff
Scruff } (*together*) Right!
Duke I want to be sure that I get my rightful share.
Ruff
Scruff } (*together*) Right!
Ruff What is your rightful share?
Duke All of it! Ha-ha-ha-ha-ha!
Ruff
Scruff } (*together*) Right!

Scruff What about our share?
Duke Your share?
Ruff ⎱ (*together*) Yes.
Scruff ⎰
Duke Well, if we find the treasure, I might be disposed to be generous. I mean, I believe I am a little behind——
Scruff Not so much a little behind as a big fat bum——
Duke — a little behind with your wages, I meant!
Ruff Only about three years.
Duke Quite. Well, I think I could see my way clear to paying you some of that...
Ruff I see.
Duke We'll discuss the details when I've — when we've — got the treasure. For now, just get moving! Go! (*Turning and pointing the way, straddling the bough as he does so*)
Ruff ⎱ (*together*) Right!
Scruff ⎰

They pick up the bough smartly, catching the Duke in the groin. He yells, they yell, drop the bough on their feet again. All yell and hop

Duke You bunglers! Leave that thing here!
Ruff We can't do that.
Duke Why not?
Scruff It's the end of the scene.
Duke So?
Ruff So at the end of the scene we have to take a bough!
Ruff ⎱ (*together*) Boom, boom!
Scruff ⎰

They take the bough and run off

Scene 6

ALONE!

The Duke is alone on stage

Duke Grrr! Cheeky devils! Wanting a share of the treasure just because they're doing all the work! Who do they think they are — taxpayers? No! They can lead me to the treasure and then... (*Making a cut-throat gesture*) Ha-ha-ha-ha! You know, all this scheming and cheating

Act II, Scene 6   55

really tires you out. What I need is something soft and warm to sink into——

Mother Hubbard enters behind him

He leans back and Mother Hubbard is there to enfold him

Hubbard Hi!
Duke (*having second thoughts*) Aaah!
Hubbard You know, Duke, I was beginning to think you were trying to give me the slip——
Duke Perish the thought. Oh, goodness, what's that?
Hubbard What's what? (*She looks away*)

The Duke runs off

I can't see any — oi! (*Going down to the audience and talking to them*) Look at that, he's run off and left me all alone, in this creepy forest, with no-one to protect me! (*Talking like a little girl*) I'm so scared! (*Suddenly changing to a glutinous TV presenter's voice*) But do you know what I do when I feel scared? I sing a song! I bet you never guessed that was coming. But I do — and it's not just any song, oh no! This is a very special song and to sing it properly, I need the help of about (*making a quick survey of the audience*) 200 people! I bet you'd never guessed that was coming either.

Music No 8

(*Speaking*) Thank you everyone, I feel so much better now. And I don't know what I was worried about really, I mean if there was any danger about you'd tell me wouldn't you? Wouldn't you?

A Mookling appears US

The audience reacts

What? Something behind me? Are you sure? All right, I'll have a look!

She looks R *and the Mookling moves to* L *keeping out of her sight. As it does so*

A second Mookling joins it

Old Mother Hubbard comes back to C

There's nothing there!

The audience say there is as the Mooklings make faces

All right, I'll look the other way.

Repeat business to the left and the Mooklings are joined by a third. Old Mother Hubbard comes back to CS

There's nothing there either!

More Mooklings enter upstage and make faces

The audience warns her again

Oh very well, if you say so, I'll try once more ...

She does a complete circle with the Mooklings circling and menacing her from behind

There's nothing there at all!

The audience insist there is as the Mooklings move down and assemble round her

No there isn't — I've looked all round in every direction ... (*Turning to the assembled Mooklings*) Haven't I!
Mooklings Oh yes!
Hubbard (*to audience*) See? (*Realizing*) Aaah!
Mooklings Aaaaah!

All flee in all directions

Scene 7

POLLY ESCAPES

Hepzibah enters, dragging Polly and followed by Astrophe (minus her tail)

Polly Stop! Let me go! I demand to know where you're taking me!
Hepzibah I told you — we're going to the lost palace of Arwon!
Polly But you said Dick sent you!

Hepzibah I lied.
Polly Why?
Astrophe She's a liar.
Hepzibah Shut up! (*To Polly*) The truth is I'm a film producer. Yes. I'm auditioning for a pure, young maiden and you've got the part. You are a pure, young maiden, aren't you?
Polly How dare you!
Hepzibah Just checking.
Polly What is all this about maidens anyway?
Hepzibah You'll find out!
Polly Tell me!
Astrophe It's quite simple. She means that she needs a maiden to feed to the great Mookie so the Mookie will grant her dearest wish which is to look like Little Witch Barbie and become the Grand Panjandrum and queen of all the witchy-poo persons.
Hepzibah No!
Astrophe In that case I haven't the faintest idea what she's on about.
Hepzibah I don't want to look like Little Witch Barbie! Who'd want to look like her? No, when the Mookie looks down at me and asks me what I want, I shall smile winningly and say: I want to look exactly like (*name of current pop diva*)

The Mooklings appear, laughing

Aaah!

Cloaca appears with a thunderclap

Aaaah!
Cloaca What exactly is going on?
Hepzibah Oh, it's you. Well ...
Cloaca (*noticing Polly*) Ha! What have we here?
Hepzibah This is the maiden! As per order.
Polly Look here——
Cloaca Silence! (*Walking round Polly*) Oh yes. She'll do very well ...
Hepzibah Do you think the Mookie will like her?
Cloaca I'm sure he'll find her — delicious! Ha-ha-ha-ha!

All cackle. Polly seizes the opportunity to stamp first on Hepzibah's foot and then on Cloaca's. They hop about.

Polly escapes

Aaaah! After her! After her!

The Mooklings stream off after Polly

Where's HP? HP! HP! That creature's up to mischief, I can feel it!

Cloaca exits

Hepzibah goes to follow but Astrophe stops her——

—— CURTAIN falls

SCENE 8

LAST CHANCE

Hepzibah You clumsy clod! Out of my way!
Astrophe No.
Hepzibah What?
Astrophe This is your last chance. Either you start acting your age and come home with me right now. Or——
Hepzibah Or what?
Astrophe — or I'm leaving you!
Hepzibah You wouldn't dare!
Astrophe Yes I would! It's the end of the line for us, the parting of the ways! The great juggernaut of life is once again about to splatter you all over its windscreen and this time I'm not going to be there to scrape you off!
Hepzibah I'll deal with you later!

Hepzibah storms off

Astrophe In your dreams, Heppy! Ah! That was good! I think I'll go home now, put my paws up and start planning a wonderful witchless future. Today is the first day of the rest of my lives!

Hepzibah exits happily, in the opposite direction

SCENE 9

FRIENDS

Scruff trudges on carrying Ruff on his back

Act II, Scene 9

Ruff Stop!
Scruff does so

What are we doing here?
Scruff We're looking for the lost treasure.
Ruff Why?
Scruff So the Duke can nick it.
Ruff Exactly! And when he's got it, what will be our share?
Scruff Er ...
Ruff Nix, nothing, zero and zilch!
Scruff That sounds about right.
Ruff But it's not right! Why should he exploit us? Ever since we've been working for him he's been riding on our backs!
Scruff Has he? I thought it was just you.
Ruff Let me down.
Scruff I could never let you down, Ruff.
Ruff Just put me down!

He does so

You know what I think? I think we should find the treasure before the Duke does and keep it for ourselves!
Scruff But that wouldn't be cricket!
Ruff Cricket? This is the game of life we're playing here, son! You have to be tough and ruthless. Are you with me?

Scruff thinks

Scruff No, I don't think I am.
Ruff I see. Well, so be it. It's your funeral.
Scruff Remember — the meek shall inherit the earth.
Ruff Only after the rich people have finished with it.
Scruff But suppose everybody thought like that?
Ruff Then I'd be stupid to think any other way, wouldn't I?
Scruff But——
Ruff Sorry. I've got a treasure to find. And when I do, it'll be all mine.

Ruff goes off singing 'Money, Money, Money' or something similar.

Scruff Ruff! Ruff!

Silence. Scruff turns to the audience

He's gone. That was my friend. At least, I thought he was my friend.

You know if I found a treasure, I'd share it with everybody. I suppose that's because I'm incredibly stupid. But, you know, perhaps Ruff's right. Perhaps everyone should be tough and ruthless. The trouble is I'm more of your rough and toothless. What do you think I should do? (*Coming to a decision*) No! I've made up my mind. Why should I be poor when they're all rich? I'll find that treasure and keep the lot! That'll teach 'em!

He exits

The deep rumbling noise is heard as the CURTAIN *opens on*

SCENE 10

THE PALACE OF ARWON

A ruined and overgrown palace courtyard

USC *is a moss-covered wall with a closed double door in it. Around the stage are three pillars and/or statues in various stages of disrepair. Cobwebs and a soft mist hang over all*

Polly runs on. She is still trying to get away from Cloaca

Polly Oh no, where am I now? Some kind of old ruined palace? Hey, this must be it — the lost palace of Arwon! I've found it! But where's the treasure? Dick said everything was made of gold and diamonds but it doesn't look like gold to me. I hope we haven't come all this way for nothing!

Sound of voices off

Oh help, that must be Cloaca and the witch!

Polly runs off

HP enters followed by Dick and Woolly

Dick Where are we? Is this it? The palace of Arwon?

HP nods

At last! Did you hear that, Woolly? Now to find the treasure!

Act II, Scene 10

Woolly Woof, woof.
Dick You still think it's a trap?
Woolly Woof, woof!
Dick No, we'll look for Polly in a minute — after I've found the treasure!

Dick starts to look for treasure. Woolly sniffs around and picks up Polly's scent. He barks to attract Dick's attention

Woolly Woof, woof!
Dick Quiet, Woolly!
Woolly Woof, woof!
Dick In a minute I said!

Woolly glares at him and then goes off in the same direction as Polly, following the scent closely

HP is very anxious

It has to be here somewhere — it has to be! (*He searches feverishly*)

Cloaca, Hepzibah and some Mooklings enter quietly

HP mews in alarm

What? — Who are you?
Cloaca Never mind. Who are you?
Hepzibah It's the boy! He was with the girl!
Dick What's going on? Where's the treasure?
Cloaca Where's the girl?
Dick I don't know——
Cloaca We'll see about that! Take him away!

A couple of Mooklings grab Dick

Dick (*to HP*) You treacherous little beast! Woolly was right — it was a trap!

HP moans and tries to deny this. The Mooklings cackle madly

Some Mookling drag Dick off

Cloaca You others keep looking for the girl!

The other Mooklings leave

Thank you, HP, well done.

HP moans

What? You didn't mean to help me? You were trying to help him?

HP nods and moans

Well, I believe you. But the boy doesn't. He thinks you betrayed him. Let that be your punishment! Ha-ha-ha-ha!

HP staggers off, moaning in despair

Hepzibah Er, excuse me.
Cloaca I've tried to but I find it almost impossible.
Hepzibah I mean — how much longer do I have to wait for my reward?
Cloaca What reward?
Hepzibah My reward for finding the girl!
Cloaca But you haven't found her. You've lost her.
Hepzibah But!——
Cloaca If you want the reward you'd better be the one who finds her again!
Hepzibah That's not fair!
Cloaca So? Ha-ha-ha-ha!

Cloaca sweeps off

Hepzibah Curses and catspaws! Sybil said she was mean, but...! (*Calling sweetly*) Girlie, where are you? Come to aunty Hepzibah — she only wants to feed you to a Mookie!

Hepzibah exits

Scene 11

AN UNLIKELY ALLIANCE

Woolly, head down, sniffing, enters. He looks up, realises he is back where he started and growls. Then he looks off and hides quickly.

Astrophe enters

Astrophe (*to audience*) All right, I know I was going to leave her but I can't. I've tried and I can't do it. I had to come back. Daft old witch!

I'm all she's got, you see. And she's all I've got. Pathetic, isn't it? Anyway — yow!

Woolly has appeared and is about to pounce. They shape up to fight but stop

Miaow.
Woolly Woof.
Astrophe No. My heart's not in it either.
Woolly Woof.
Astrophe Lost my mistress, you see.
Woolly Woof.
Astrophe You too, eh?
Woolly Woof.
Astrophe Bit of a bummer, eh.
Woolly (*nodding, woofing the line, sadly*) To be or not to be, that is the question
Astrophe No, it's not. The question is what are we going to do about it?
Woolly Woof! Woof!

Woolly scratches Astrophe's back then offers his own to be scratched

Astrophe You'll help me if I'll help you?

They spit and shake paws

Done!

Woolly returns Astrophe's tail

Thank you. How do humans get themselves in these messes?

They hurry off together

SCENE 12

THE GREAT MOOKIE!

Old Mother Hubbard enters cautiously

Hubbard Yuk! What a disgusting old ruin. And speaking of disgusting old ruins, I wonder what's happened to the Duke. Fancy running off like that and leaving me all alone in this awful place!

A noise off

A noise off! Someone's coming! I must hide!

She hides behind a pillar or statue

The Duke enters angrily

Duke Grrr! I've searched every inch of this place and haven't found so much as a pinch of gold dust!
Hubbard (*aside*) It's the Duke!
Duke The only luck I've had all day is getting rid of the old woman!
Hubbard (*aside*) Old woman? Who can he mean?
Duke That Old Mother Hubbard!
Hubbard (*aside*) Oh, that's who he means. (*Realizing*) What! (*She is about to step out and confront him*)
Duke But not a sign of my treasure!
Hubbard (*aside*) His treasure! He means my little Polly ...
Duke I've got to find that boy!
Hubbard (*aside*) Boy?
Duke There's a heap of treasure here and only he knows where it is!
Hubbard (*aside*) Treasure?
Duke Gold!
Hubbard (*aside*) Gold?
Duke Jewels!
Hubbard (*aside*) Jewels!

The Duke looks round suspiciously but before he can see her a noise comes from offstage

Hubbard ⎫
Duke   ⎬ (*together*) Aaah! Someone's coming!
Duke It could be the boy!
Hubbard (*aside*) I'm getting very worried about him.

The Duke runs to hide behind another statue

Ruff enters as the Duke and Old Mother Hubbard peer out from behind their statues

Ruff Oh no, this place goes on for ever!
Hubbard (*aside*) Ruff? What's he doing here?
Duke (*aside*) He's still looking for the treasure! Good boy! (*The Duke is about to greet Ruff*)
Ruff (*to audience*) I've got to find that treasure before the Duke does!
Duke (*aside*) What's this?

Act II, Scene 12   65

Ruff He might be 'disposed to be generous'. Ha! In a pig's ear he might!
Duke (*aside*) He doesn't trust me!
Ruff I don't trust him.
Duke (*aside*) He's quite right.
Ruff I know I am! (*Realizing*) What——?

He is about to investigate when he is distracted by a noise off

All Aaaah! Someone's coming!

Ruff runs and hides

Scruff enters

Scruff (*to audience*) The more I think about it Ruff was quite right. If you can't beat 'em — join 'em!
Ruff (*aside*) Good man! (*He is about to step out*)
Scruff Only I shall take it a step further ...
Ruff (*aside*) Eh?
Scruff I will beat 'em ...
Ruff (*aside*) Eh??
Scruff But I won't join 'em!
Ruff (*aside*) The treacherous little devil!
Scruff I've got a new motto: do unto others before they do it unto me!

Scruff makes to go but Ruff steps out

Ruff Aha!
Scruff Aaaah!
Ruff Well may you cringe away so guilty-like! Double-cross me, would you? And I thought we were friends! I thought we trusted each other! I thought we were blood brothers and bosom buddies but all this time I've been nursing a viper under my wing! No — don't touch me!
Scruff But ...
Ruff I'd always intended to share the treasure with you but after this, well, it just wouldn't be right! I'm afraid that now I have no choice but to punish you by keeping it all for myself!
Scruff But ...
Ruff Such treachery! What would the Duke say?
Duke (*stepping out*) He'd say you were no better than he is.
Ruff \
Scruff / (*together*) Aaah!
Duke You're both treacherous dogs!
Ruff I can explain——!

Scruff It was all his fault——!
Ruff (*to Scruff*) Shut up! (*To Duke*) There's no need to be angry...
Duke Angry? Angry? I'm too sad to be angry. I thought there was an understanding between us — trust, respect, nay love even! But now, after this betrayal, I couldn't possibly share the treasure with you! Oh woe, woe — who would have thought it!
Hubbard (*stepping out*) Well, I would have for one!
All Aaaah!
Hubbard What a prize parcel of rogues you are! I thought you came here to help me save Polly but now I discover all you're interested in is some old treasure! And what is treasure anyway?

Cloaca enters behind them

Cloaca It's this ... (*She raises her arm and with a scatter of glitter casts a spell*)

Magic music

Brightly shining jewels appear everywhere. (Christmas tree lights can be used but a mirror ball may be the best way to achieve this effect)

All (*entranced by greed*) The treasure! ...
Cloaca Yes! Diamonds bright as knives, pearls like poison, emeralds green as envy and rubies red as hate! ...
All Aaaah!
Cloaca And it's all yours——
All Mine!

Cloaca claps her hands. The jewels vanish

Cloaca When you find me a maiden!
All What?
Ruff Where are we going to find one of those?
Scruff In a place like this?
Hubbard It's impossible!
Duke They're like policemen——
All There's never one there when you need one!

Polly runs in, pursued by Hepzibah. Polly stops when she sees the assembled multitude

Polly Mother! Duke! Ruff and Scruff!

Act II, Scene 12   67

All Polly!

They all move in on her, each intent on using her to gain the treasure for themselves

Hepzibah Hands off — she's mine!
Hubbard Yours? She's my daughter! The treasure's mine!
Duke She's my fiancée! The treasure's mine!
Scruff He doesn't even love her!
Ruff He only wanted to marry her so he'd get all the housework done for nothing!
Ruff
Scruff } (*together*) The treasure's ours for being made redundant!

They all begin to squabble violently, pulling Polly to and fro

Polly Mother—! Stop it! What's happened to you all?

Cloaca laughs and snaps her fingers

  The Mooklings bring Dick in with his hands tied together

One Mookling sets a stake C while other Mooklings seize Polly and bind her to the stake

Polly Dick——!
Dick Polly, my dearest——!
All She's not yours — she's mine!

They start to squabble again

Cloaca You're all wrong! She's mine!
All What——?
Cloaca Or rather, the great Mookie's!
All The great Mookie?

There's a thunderclap and flash of lightning and then comes a great rumbling roar

Cloaca The Mookie awakes! Back! Back!

All retreat from the great doors. Polly struggles but cannot move. Dick struggles to help her but is restrained by Mooklings. The doors begin to open and the head of the Mookie appears. It is huge and evil with shining eyes and a great dragon-like mouth that opens and closes. Flames and smoke swirl around. All shriek in terror

Dick Somebody help her! That monster's going to eat Polly!
All Aaaah!

They are paralyzed by fear

Polly Help! Dick! Mother!
Dick Will nobody raise a hand to save her?!

Woolly appears dramatically at one side and Astrophe at the other

Woolly Woof!
Astrophe Meow!
Dick Woolly——!
Hepzibah You——!
Astrophe Untie the girl, Woolly! I'll deal with this lot!

Woolly runs to the stake and begins trying to untie Polly

Cloaca Mooklings — deal with that creature!

A couple of Mooklings move in and attack Woolly. He struggles to beat them off as he tries to free Polly. The Mookie continues to snap and roar

Fight music

Astrophe takes on all comers with great bravado. Astrophe eventually overcomes all the Mooklings but in her moment of triumph is knocked out cold by the vengeful witch who has been stalking her during the fight

Hepzibah Ha!
Cloaca Get the dog! The dog!

The Mooklings all rise and — possibly in slow motion — advance on Woolly and Polly. Woolly realizes he has lost and has no options left. He pushes Polly towards Dick who has broken free and then throws himself into the Mookie's mouth. The jaws slam shut. Cloaca gives a terrible scream of despair

  Aaaah!

Act II, Scene 12

The Mookie makes a fearsome roaring sound. Its eyes roll, its head thrashes about. After a final huge spasm it dies

The Mookie — It's dead! — That creature has killed my Mookie!

Cloaca staggers off, grieving

Sad music

There is a pause. Then the Mookie's mouth opens. The figure of prince Lorien crawls out

Lorien Free! Free!
Dick What? What's going on? Who are you?
Lorien I am Lorien, last Prince of Arwon!

All gasp

Polly Prince Lorien?
Dick The one who was turned into a monster?
Lorien Yes.
Polly You mean that was you?
Lorien Yes, I was the great Mookie.
Polly But what about your princess? Where is she?
Lorien Cloaca turned her into a monster too and kept her always by her side. She had to stand by and watch the evil things Cloaca made her poor prince do. She was her Hidden Princess so she called her HP.
Hubbard HP? What a sauce!
Polly Where is she now?

HP enters, a monster no longer but wearing a beautiful wedding gown and looking like a picture

HP I am here!

All gasp

Lorien Angelina!
HP Lorien!
Lorien At last!
HP The spell is broken!

They embrace, kiss

Polly But what broke it?
HP Your dog.
Dick Woolly?
HP Yes.
Polly How did he do that?
Lorien There's only one thing in the world powerful enough to break a spell like this one.
Polly What's that?
HP A good deed. An act of unselfish love. Woolly loved you so much he was willing to die to save your life.
Hubbard Poor Woolly ...
Lorien And he broke the spell on all of you as well.
All Spell? On us?
HP (*to Ruff*) Would you really not have shared the treasure with your friend?
Ruff No!
Scruff Never!

They embrace

HP And, Mother Hubbard, would you really have allowed your daughter to be hurt just so that you could be rich?
Hubbard Of course not! But I was going to, wasn't I? Oh, Polly, can you ever forgive me?
Polly I already have. Mother, I know Dick is still poor but I do love him. Please give us your blessing.
Hubbard Of course! Dick...
Dick Mother!

All three embrace.

Hepzibah is weeping over the body of Astrophe

Lorien What about you, Hepzibah? Did you really mean to hurt your cat who was so faithful to you?
Hepzibah No, no! Oh, Astrophe! Wake up! Wake up!
Astrophe (*waking up*) Uh?
Hepzibah She lives!
Astrophe What happened? Where am I?
Hepzibah You're in mumsy-wumsy's arms and that's where you're going to stay!
Astrophe Have you been sniffing the Araldite again?
Hepzibah No! I have seen the light! We're going to settle down quietly, you and I, and live happily ever after!

Astrophe Do you mean that?
Hepzibah Yes!

Hepzibah kisses Astrophe

Duke This is wonderful! Everywhere I look I see beauty!
Hubbard Oh? Do you? (*Approching the Duke*) Er, Duke?
Duke Yes?
Hubbard I think it's best if Polly marries Dick, don't you?
Duke Oh yes, of course!
Hubbard But that still leaves you, doesn't it?
Duke Yes ...
Hubbard All alone up there in that vast castle ...
Duke Yes ...
Hubbard With all that money ....
Duke Yes ...
Hubbard Whatever will you do?
Duke I don't know. Unless——
Hubbard Yes?
Duke — I hardly dare suggest it——
Hubbard Dare, dare!
Duke — well, unless you would condescend to share it with me?
Hubbard Oh Duke! I thought you'd never ask!

They embrace warmly

Polly This is the happiest day of my life!
Dick And it's all thanks to Woolly ...
Polly Poor, noble Woolly!

Ruff and Scruff have retrieved the body of Woolly from the Mookie's mouth. Now they carry it reverently down C. They lay it down and all gather round in sorrow

Lorien A noble animal indeed.

Soft music under

> He must be buried here in the heart of the city he saved. And we will build a monument of marble and place it over his grave and every year, on the anniversary of this day, there will be a public holiday and dogs will come from all parts of the kingdom to Woolly's tomb and — pay their respects!

Woolly (*suddenly sitting up, not entirely happy with this last idea*) Woof, woof!

All Woolly! You're alive!
Woolly Woof, woof!

There is much rejoicing with Woolly slobbering over everybody

Ruff So in fact there wasn't really any lost treasure of Arwon after all.
Lorien If you mean gold, silver and diamonds, no. That was just Cloaca's evil magic. But you've all found a greater treasure here — the treasure of true love. And that's a treasure everyone can share.

Lorien embraces HP. The Duke embraces Old Mother Hubbard. Dick and Woolly embrace Polly. Hepzibah embraces Astrophe. Ruff embraces Scruff

Hubbard There's only one thing I'd like now ...
Lorien What's that, Mother Hubbard? Your wish is my command!
Hubbard Well, it's not for me really. It's for Woolly. You see, every day for as long as I can remember, I've been going to that rotten old cupboard of mine and finding it bare! I would like, just once, to be able to offer Woolly a bone and actually give him one!
Lorien That's easily done. Hepzibah ...
Hepzibah With pleasure! (*She waves her wand*)

A chord of music

A huge bone appears with a bow round it and lights flashing

All cheer

The Chorus enter

Music No 9 (Finale)

CURTAIN

FURNITURE AND PROPERTY LIST
ACT I
Scene 1

Off stage: Party whistles etc. (**Witches, warlocks and monstrosities**)
Placard reading: Hepzibah for queen (**Astrophe**)

Personal: Electric frog-squeezer (**Queen Mavis**)
Two envelopes (**MC**)

Scene 2

Personal: Large Mars Bar with a mouse tail hanging out (**Astrophe**)

Scene 3

On stage: Trees, wishing wells

Scene 4

Off stage: Fishing rod (**Old Mother Hubbard**)
Elastic dog lead attached to a stuffed dog (**Stage Management**)
Basket of flowers (**Polly**)

Scene 5

No additional props required

Scene 6

Off stage: An extraordinary vehicle (**Duke, Ruff and Scruff**)
A large, heavy parcel (**Ruff and Scruff**)
A huge axe (**Dick**)

Scene 7

No additional props required

Scene 8

Off stage: Phone (**Hepzibah**)

Scene 9

On stage: Stool
Easel with implements

Off stage:	Tray of sandwiches (**Sybil**)
	Youth Machine *In it*: a baby in a shawl with a tiny pointed hat (**Two dolly birds**)
Personal:	Baby's dummy (**Hepzibah**)

SCENE 10

Personal:	Wand (**Hepzibah**)

SCENE 11

On stage:	Scruffy carpet or dust cover
	Four buckets of water
	Two buckets of torn up paper
Off stage:	Assorted boxes sized small to large (**Servants**)
	Box. *In it:* Wallpaper (a length of painted stage canvas), paste, Polyfilla, bucket, pasting brush

ACT II

SCENE 1

On stage:	Magical, mysterious forest

SCENE 2

No additional props required

SCENE 3

No additional props required

SCENE 4

Off stage:	Astrophe's tail (**Woolly**)

SCENE 5

Off stage:	A long bough like a lance (**Scruff**)

SCENE 6

No additional props required

SCENE 7

No additional props required

Furniture and Property List

Scene 8

No additional props required

Scene 9

No additional props required

Scene 10

On stage: Ruined and overgrown palace courtyard
A moss covered wall with a double door in it. *Behind it:* The Mookie - a dragon like head with rolling eyes and snapping jaws
Three ruined pillars or statues
Cobwebs

Scene 11

No additional props required

Scene 12

Off stage: A stake **(One Mookling)**

Personal: Glitter **(Cloaca)**

LIGHTING PLOT

Practical fittings required: glitter ball, strobe
Various interior and exterior settings

ACT I, Scene 1

Cue 1	**Witches, warlocks, MC, etc.** erupt into auditorium *House lights or auditorium lighting*	(Page 1)
Cue 2	**MC** steps forward *Follow spot*	(Page 1)
Cue 3	**Queen Mavis** enters auditorium *Follow spot*	(Page 1)
Cue 4	**Little Witch Barbie** enters auditorium *Follow spot*	(Page 2)
Cue 5	**Hepzibah and Astrophe** enter auditorium *Follow spot*	(Page 2)
Cue 6	**Hepzibah and Astrophe** make their way to the tabs as everyone else leaves the auditorium. *Cross fade house lights or auditorium lighting to tab lighting and fade spot*	(Page 3)

ACT I, Scene 2

To open: Tab lights

Cue 7	**Hepzibah and Astrophe** exit *Take out tab lights*	(Page 4)

ACT I, Scene 3

To open: Bright general rural exterior lighting

No cues

ACT I, Scene 4

To open: Continues from previous scene

Lighting Plot

Cue 8	**Old Mother Hubbard** appears at the rear of the auditorium *Follow spot, then fade out as she reaches the stage*	(Page 6)
Cue 9	**Woolly** appears in the auditorium *Follow spot, as Woolly and Hubbard interact with audience then fade out when they return to the stage*	(Page 7)
Cue 10	**Polly** appears in the auditorium *Follow spot, than fade out as she reaches the stage*	(Page 10)

ACT I, SCENE 5

To open: Warm romantic lighting

Cue 11	**Hubbard, Polly and Woolly** sing Music No 2 *Follow spot*	(Page 11)
Cue 12	End of Music No 2 *Take out spot*	(Page 11)
Cue 13	**Villagers** come rushing on *Bright, general rural exterior lighting*	(Page 12)

ACT I, SCENE 6

To open: Bright general rural exterior lighting

Cue 14	**Dick** appears and poses heroically *Follow spot briefly then fade out*	(Page 17)
Cue 15	**Hubbard, Duke, Ruff, Scruff and Chorus** sing Music No 3 *Follow spot*	(Page 19)
Cue 16	End of Music No 3 *Take out spot*	(Page 19)

ACT I, SCENE 7

To open: Continues from previous scene

Cue 17	**Hubbard.** "Kill! Kill!" *Sinister lighting and follow spot as Woolly transforms*	(Page 20)

into a vicious, snarling hound and advances on the peasants, then take out spot and revert to previous lighting when he changes back to normal

Cue 18   **Dick** "...That's what men are for." *He poses heroically*   (Page 22)
Follow spot on **Dick** *then fade out as* CURTAIN *closes*

ACT I, SCENE 8

To open: Cross-fade to tab lighting

No cues

ACT I, SCENE 9

To open: Cross-fade to Sybil's Necromantic Parlour as the CURTAIN opens
    General interior lighting

Cue 19   **Leonardo and Sybil** "...The Youth Machine!"   (Page 25)
Follow spot on two **Dolly Birds** *as they enter with the Youth Machine, fade out on dialogue*

ACT I, SCENE 10

To open: Cross-fade to tab lighting

Cue 20   **Hepzibah and Astrophe** sing Music No 4   (Page 28)
Follow spot

Cue 21   End of Music No 4   (Page 28)
Take out spot

ACT I, SCENE 11

To open: Cross-fade as the CURTAIN opens on a dingy room in the Duke's castle

Cue 22   **Ruff and Scruff** pursue the **Duke** into the auditorium   (Page 35)
Follow spot

Cue 23   **Duke** "Idiots! Get this mess cleared up before ——"   (Page35)
Take out spot

Lighting Plot

ACT I, SCENE 12

To open: Cross-fade to tab lighting

No cues

ACT I, SCENE 13

To open: Cross-fade to the Kingdom of Love
Warm, romantic lighting

Cue 24	**Dick, Polly, Woolly and Chorus** sing Music No 5 *Follow spot*	(Page 38)
Cue 25	End of Music No 5 *Take out spot*	(Page 38)
Cue 26	The CURTAIN slowly closes *Fade lights to Black-out*	(Page 38)

ACT II, SCENE 1

To open: Magical, mysterious forest lighting

Cue 27	**Mooklings and Forest Creatures** dance to Music No 6 *Follow spot*	(Page 39)
Cue 28	End of Music No 6 *Take out spot*	(Page 39)

ACT II, SCENE 2

To open: Continues from previous scene

Cue 29	**Cloaca and Mooklings** sing Music No 7 *Follow spot*	(Page 43)
Cue 30	End of Music No 7 *Take out spot*	(Page 43)

ACT II, SCENE 3

To open: Continues from previous scene

No cues

ACT II, Scene 4

To open: Continues from previous scene

No cues

ACT II, Scene 5

To open: Continues from previous scene

No cues

ACT II, Scene 6

To open: Continues from previous scene

| *Cue* 31 | **Hubbard, Chorus and Audience** sing Music No 8
Follow spot | (Page 55) |
| *Cue* 32 | End of Music No 8
Take out spot | (Page 55) |

ACT II, Scene 7

To open: Continues from previous scene

No cues

ACT II, Scene 8

To open: Cross-fade to tab lighting

No cues

ACT II, Scene 9

To open: Continues from previous scene

No cues

Lighting Plot

ACT II, SCENE 10

To open: Cross-fade as the CURTAIN opens on a ruined and overgrown palace courtyard
Bright, general outside lighting

No cues

ACT II, SCENE 11

To open: Continues from previous scene

No cues

ACT II, SCENE 12

To open: Continues from previous scene

Cue 33	**Cloaca** "it's this ..." *Mirror ball or fairy lights for jewel effect*	(Page 66)
Cue 34	**All** "Mine" Cloaca claps her hands *Take out mirror ball or fairy lights*	(Page 66)
Cue 35	**All** "The Great Mookie?" *Lightning flash*	(Page 67)
Cue 36	**Cloaca** "Get the dog! The dog!" *Strobe for slow motion effect on chase until* **Cloaca** *gives a terrible scream of despair*	(Page 68)
Cue 37	**Company** sings Music No 9 *Follow spot*	(Page 72)
Cue 38	End of Music No 9 *Take out spot*	(Page 72)
Cue 39	CURTAIN *Fade lights to Black-out*	(Page 72)

EFFECTS PLOT

ACT I

Cue 1	**Ruff and Scruff** drop the parcel *A huge amplified crash*	(Page 14)
Cue 2	**Ruff and Scruff** drop the parcel again *A huge amplified crash*	(Page 15)
Cue 3	**Duke** drops the parcel *A huge crash*	(Page 15)
Cue 4	**Astrophe** knocks on the curtain *A huge echoing knocking sound*	(Page 22)
Cue 5	**Astrophe** knocks on the curtain again *A loud oink followed by a crash*	(Page 23)
Cue 6	**Sybil** (*off*) "Go away! I'm busy!" *A huge oink followed by a crash*	(Page 23)
Cue 7	**Sybil** (*off*) "Can't talk now ..." *An oink followed by a crash*	(Page 23)
Cue 8	**Sybil** (*off*) "Not to me!" *An oink followed by a crash*	(Page 23)
Cue 9	**Sybil** indicates to Dolly Birds where to press the button *Bubbling noise, music and smoke everywhere*	(Page 26)
Cue 10	**Sybil** opens a flap in the machine *Sound of a baby crying*	(Page 26)
Cue 11	**Sybil** puts the baby into the machine *Bubbling noise, music and smoke everywhere*	(Page 26)
Cue 12	**Hepzibah** "... transport us to the old lost palace!" *A flash and a bang*	(Page 29)
Cue 13	**Dick, Polly and Woolly** link arms and set off *Rose petals and hearts fall*	(Page 38)

Effects Plot

ACT II

Cue 14	The Mookling ballet ends *Deep rumbling sound*	(Page 39)
Cue 15	**Polly** "No, that rumbling noise———" *Deep rumbling sound*	(Page 39)
Cue 16	To open Scene 2 *Alternating thumps and miaows*	(Page 39)
Cue 17	**Hepzibah** "... you horrible little beast!" *Thunderclap*	(Page 40)
Cue 18	**Cloaca** "But I suggest you hurry———" *Deep rumbling sound*	(Page 42)
Cue 19	End of Song 7 *Deep rumbling sound*	(Page 43)
Cue 20	**Old Mother Hubbard** "Listen!" *Deep rumbling sound*	(Page 44)
Cue 21	**Old Mother Hubbard** "... an old pioneer." *Dinosaur-type roaring off stage*	(Page 45)
Cue 22	**Scruff** "Wow! Something really scared them" *Dinosaur-type roaring off stage*	(Page 45)
Cue 23	To open Scene 4 *Deep rumbling sound*	(Page 46)
Cue 24	**Hepzibah** "Aaah!" (First time) *Thunderclap as* **Cloaca** *appears*	(Page 57)
Cue 25	To open Scene 10 *Deep rumbling sound - A soft mist effect*	(Page 60)
Cue 26	**Cloaca** "It's this ..." (*She raises her arm*) *Magic music*	(Page 66)
Cue 27	**All** "The great Mookie?" *Thunderclap*	(Page 67)
Cue 28	The head of the Mookie appears *Flames and smoke swirl around*	(Page 671)

Cue 29	**Cloaca** "Mooklings — deal with that creature!" *Fight music*	(Page 68)
Cue 30	**Cloaca** "...That creature has killed my Mookie!" *Sad music*	(Page 69)
Cue 31	**Lorien** "A noble animal indeed" *Soft music*	(Page 71)
Cue 32	**Hepzibah** "With pleasure!" (*Waving her wand*) *Huge bone appears with a bow round it and lights flashing*	(Page 72)

www.ingramcontent.com/pod-product-compliance
Ingram Content Group UK Ltd.
Pitfield, Milton Keynes, MK11 3LW, UK
UKHW021844210426
5322IPUK00022B/451